Praise for Ho**[...]**

"How To Listen Out Loud is an absolutely delightful read. Personal, engaging, intelligent and eminently practical, author Lauren Powers takes us on a step-by-step journey into the vital skills of effective listening and communication. In a world rife with divisiveness, blame and 'othering', this book offers a sound path back to harmony in all our relationships. A must read for anyone who leads, works with or wants to connect more deeply with people."

— Karen Kimsey-House, Co-Founder and Board Chair,
The Co-Active Training Institute and coauthor of
Co-Active Leadership and *Co-Active Coaching*

"There are books that offer some interesting learning points and then there are books that really change things. Lauren's brilliant insights into the art and science of listening will transform the way you communicate. This is the go-to book if you are interested in having every aspect of your life (and our world) be better… Listening fixes (almost) everything! Lauren offers what is needed most in our world right now: real tangible tools for positive lasting change."

— Rick Tamlyn, MCC, Hay House author of
Play Your Bigger Game and founder of Produce U

"Our wonderful brains offer countless reasons to listen to our own thoughts and brilliant ideas more than to other people. Lauren Powers goes after all of these distractions like an Olympic whack-a-mole player. She nails what it takes to listen well and offers us ways to practice and grow muscle to really listen. If you want your relationships, friendships and work to flourish, this is your next step."

— Cynthia Loy Darst, CPCC, ORSCC, MCC,
author of *Meet Your Inside Team*

"Put this book on your required reading list! Radiant with humor, *How to Listen Out Loud* delivers the magic formula to transform and evolve personal and workplace relationships using one tool — listening. Buckle up, though; Lauren Powers' ingenious narrative, comical examples, and invitations for skill development teach us a new perspective. One that will help us 'think through, feel through, and live through this life together' in a richer and more textured way."

— Zoe-Ann Bartlett, Founder of Intentional Table and author of *If I Had a Daughter*

"Lauren Powers has written an essential guide to the one skill we all think we know about but somehow don't do effectively: listening! With her signature humor and deep insight, she teaches us the skills and mindsets we need to connect with each other more deeply, learn and retain information, and ultimately change our perspectives and worlds. I loved every word. Yes, this book will make you a better listener and in doing so, a better human. For that reason, I use Powers' *How To Listen Out Loud* training inside the DEI programs my organization provides to corporate leaders."

— Priya Nalkur, EdD, Founder and President of the RoundTable Institute

"Lauren Powers has done the impossible: written a book about listening that had me laughing out loud. In this fast-paced, smart, and hilarious book she covers everything we need to know about listening. Why we're not good at it, how we can get great at it, and what is possible when we do. It is a light read that goes deep and has changed the way I listen for good."

— Mary Reynolds Thompson, author of *Reclaiming the Wild Soul* and *A Wild Soul Woman*

"*How To Listen Out Loud* does not tell you what you should do, as much as it invites you to embrace what you can do for yourself, and others. It's not a self-help book. It's a self-awareness book. Lauren has found just the right balance of humor, insight, and encouragement to make the material accessible and attainable. The Play Date exercises are fabulous!"

— Rodney Smith, Playwright, *Full-Tilt Boogie at the Big Bang Diner*

"In an era of ever-growing culture wars, we are lonelier, more isolated, and hungrier to be listened to than ever before. Enter *How to Listen Out Loud*, with a crucial new piece to the puzzle: good listening includes talking! Filled with humor and a can-do spirit, this book connects the dots that other listening approaches have failed to do. Powers, a top-notch researcher in brain science and empathy, breaks her knowledge down into simple ways to improve your listening and speaking skills, and peppers the book with hilarious anecdotes, cutting-edge data, and tell-all confessionals. A must read."

— Jeff Jacobson, author of *The Broom Closet Stories*

"Lauren Powers is an extraordinarily gifted coach, trainer, writer and performer. In her new book, *Listening Out Loud*, Lauren shows her ability to convey knowledge and wisdom with wit and substance. She also looks at the art of communicating from the viewpoint of developing the skill of listening, an essential part of dialogue that sometimes takes a back seat to what we actually say. Lauren reminds us that listening is as important —and possibly more so — than talking."

— Kim Fowler, author of *All Will Be Well: A Memoir of Love and Dementia*

"In *How to Listen Out Loud*, Lauren Powers deepens our appreciation of the power of listening in fostering quality human connection and understanding. In her inviting and playful way, she presents us with valuable insights as to why we as human beings have so much trouble listening to each other and provides us with new perspectives to facilitate our ability to listen well. Lauren also gives us accessible, fun tools for mastering both the art and the gift of listening. A big shout out to *How to Listen Out Loud!*"

— Andrew L. Miser, PhD, author of *The Partnership Marriage*

How To
LISTEN
Out Loud

How To
LISTEN
Out Loud

Ridiculously Powerful Skills for Leading, Relating, & Happifying

Lauren Powers, MCC

Published by

PLUCK
publications

To contact the author about speaking, workshops or ordering books in bulk, visit www.HowtoListenOutLoud.com

ISBN (paperback): 979-8-9875994-0-2
ISBN (ebook): 979-8-9875994-1-9

Editor: Mary Reynolds Thompson
Book design: Christy Day, Constellation Book Services
Cover illustration: © Chetverikoff / Dreamstime.com
Author photos: Briana Autran Photography

Printed in the United States of America

For Joan R. Powers (1929-2007)

Contents

I Was a Champion Non-Listener

"Auntie Yang is not hard of hearing.
She is hard of listening."

–Amy Tan (American author of
The Joy Luck Club, 1952–present)

In order to fill you with confidence about my credentials, I'm supposed to wow you right here. But where I'd like to start is how bad a listener I've been in my life. All-about-me, judge-y, easily bored. Not good.

Growing up in a lineage of repressed Irish Catholics, the rule in my family was the more sarcastic the better. In my teen years I perfected the power tool of disdain, the eyeroll. By my 20s, out in the wider world, I was a pretty clear case of arrested development. My relationships, at work and with my friends and family, weren't improving, weren't deepening. As an adult, wasn't that supposed to happen?

If I got to talk about me, my ideas, my hopes, the conversation was great. Once I had run out of steam, the chat was over. Like the cartoon where two people are seated at a café table and one says to the other, "Enough about me. What do you think about me?"

Remember the old adage that if you don't have anything nice to say, then don't say it? Most of my thoughts about other people fell into this category. That limits conversation if you're not supposed to say, "The reason you're confused is you are a stupidhead." Rarely did it occur to me, to ask my conversation partner about their life. I mean, who cares? I'm busy, working hard over here trying to look smart, or cool while also judging you about your smartness and coolness.

Naturally I blamed everyone else for as long as I could. But that didn't change anything. Finally, finally, finally I had to admit that I was one-half of every single conversation I was in. Maybe I could improve something, somehow? My only option, then, was to look at myself.

Do I Have To?

For me, every one of us humans is a hero figure in this epic saga of being alive. And as you may know, all good hero's journeys start with answering the call to adventure. Helen Keller, who had good reasons to stay home and mope, said, "Life is either a daring adventure or nothing at all." That's the spirit! Even so, those calls that invite us to risk, to fail, to recover are hard to say yes to. You've got to have a really good reason to say, "I am up for the ride."

My call to become an Out Loud Listener admittedly didn't start well. Despite being no good at conversation of any depth I wanted to be a therapist. My parents had provided me with a fine, rational, keep-it-to-yourself childhood. But I harbored Out Loud feelings, romantic and artsy enthusiasms. In other words, drama.

I was into Gothic novels and black eyeliner, and curious about what makes people act the way they do. Why are most of us so boring? How can life be more like the movies? So, I chose Psychology as my major. But the early courses focused on Pavlov's drooling dog and rats pushing levers for more cocaine. Worst of all, I happened on a copy of the DSM, which is the Manual of Mental Disorders, put out by the American Psychiatric Association. The pages fell open to the description of a real, every day, murderous psychopath. I changed majors.

Several years later, in my 30s, and working as corporate trainer, I discovered the Co-Active Training Institute. The founders of CTI became my mentors. Their coaching model is based on the idea that each of us has a rich, meaningful inner life that guides our feelings, behaviors, and outcomes. The focus in coaching is not analyzing problems, neuroses, and flaws. Rather the overarching philosophy of Co-Active Coaching is that every individual is resourceful, creative, whole. That is the level on which we can engage with each other.

At first, I thought that coaching had to be some kind of California New Age Crapola. But the workshops were fun, and my employer was paying for them, so I kept attending. Talk about being in the right place at the right time. Because this approach is not any kind of fluff. This is a whole new way to think about and cultivate productive, dynamic relationships.

Humans, after only a few thousand years, are figuring out how to be better to ourselves and to each other. We've had a good run with analyzing what's wrong. (Freud, I'm looking at you.) But what if we tried focusing on what works about people? Let's build on strengths, encourage fulfillment, develop emotional intelligence, cultivate gratitude, make bold choices. That's a human party I'd like to attend.

All of that is available when you Listen Out Loud. I learned how to listen this way, as I trained, to be a coach. But the deal is, these are social interaction skills, communication skills, relationship skills. Somehow, we've relegated skillful listening to just a few careers like therapists or bartenders. Which is a clever way to let the rest of us off the hook of having to listen at all.

Listening Out Loud can be used by everyone with everyone, everywhere to fabulous effect. You will not be a therapist but rather a good listener, a good friend, a good human. Out Loud Listening is engaged, vital, satisfying. For truly, conversation is how we create our world together. How we listen and respond to other people has an important impact on the quality of all our relationships, our co-workers & clients, and our families & friends.

Most of my work depends on the quality of my listening. I am a Master Certified Coach, one of fewer, as of this writing, than 1400 in the world, thank you very much. You might imagine me, as I listen, silently nodding with a wise look on my face, an objective outsider with a clipboard. Nah. That is not what Out Loud Listening looks or sounds like. I'm asking questions, having feelings, checking in, wondering aloud, reflecting back, brainstorming. In a high-energy conversation, there's hand waving, laughing, walking around. Or in a quieter talk, leaning in, encouraging a slower pace, considering nuance & mood.

Listening well is at the heart of so much: building trust, creating connection, having influence, leading effectively, bonding with others. What really got me interested, of course, were my own feelings of satisfaction and fulfillment. Simply by Listening Out Loud, I can make a difference, I can contribute, I can add value and meaning. I'm afraid this is a convoluted way of saying that Listening Out Loud is still all about me. So be it.

Truly though, these skills will improve things. No matter where you start. Maybe you've been promoted to manage people. Perhaps an important relationship is a bit squishy right now. Or you're just kinda lonely and want to connect. All of these reasons are perfect. Because it all begins with a little whisper that says, you know... getting better at listening may make a difference here.

Being a great listener is not an inborn talent, which you probably intuited from my story. I learned to listen step-by-step, and you can too. I appreciate you joining me here to give listening the attention it deserves and to see what impact it can have for you and your life.

Naturally, we will investigate the technical steps for "how to" Listen Out Loud. Only learning the skills, though, won't take us far enough. We're also going to identify your usual habits of listening, why you have them, and new mindsets to play with that expand your capacities.

Given that I am lazy, I find it unfortunate that these skills take study and practice. You know how in the first *The Matrix* movie, Trinity gets a download and in three seconds she can fly a helicopter? I'd so give you that for listening if I could.

What I can promise is I'll do my best to keep our time together simple & straightforward. It will be a hero's journey all the same.

CHAPTER 1

It's Not Them

"One advantage of talking to yourself is that you know at least someone is listening."

-Franklin P. Jones (American reporter, 1908-1980)

I'd like to address head-on the idea that how we prove ourselves in this world is through talking. We show we're smart, we studied the stuff, we know things, we can do the job, through talking. Please don't misunderstand—I personally love talking. An Extrovert with a capital "E" over here. But many of us grow up in a world where the people who get to talk are the parents, the teachers, the bosses. What is modeled for us is that the big people with power, get to give their opinions and stories and advice. And what listening meant, in those situations, is doing what they want you to do: be obedient.

My own dad was a 30-year military officer. My mom, trying to help me survive to adulthood, would say, "just listen to your father and everything will be fine." What that meant was "do as he says, as soon as he says it." In case you're wondering, I am still working through my authority issues.

After coming of age in a world where we might have had to listen more than talk, naturally, when we get our chance to hold forth, we're going to go all out. Finally, I get to say some stuff and be paid attention to. Listen up! I am self-expressing over here!

It turns out, though, that in the same way I was not that interested in listening to my elders, people weren't that interested in hearing me. What a disappointment. Maybe if I speak more loudly? Like an American in a foreign country, yelling slowly in English thinking that will translate. Or what if I repeat myself repeatedly and over again and a lot? Or surely a sarcastic comment about their single brain cell will get their attention. Thus, I kept doing the same things hoping for a different result. Crazy-making. But I did not know any other way to approach this.

My sense is that many of us don't know how else to be in conversation. For many years, I've gotten to teach courses, all over the globe, on how to be a good listener. Everyone struggles! Managers, grandmothers, artists, nurses, lawyers, engineers, clerks, people from corporate, engineers, actors, realtors, librarians, consultants. Did I mention engineers?

Ironically, lots of us think we're already good listeners. I mean, haven't we been doing it all our lives? The fact is, no, we haven't—not true listening. There aren't many places to learn how to be better listeners either. Role models are scarce. Listening takes time and focus, which are always in short supply. And, you know, we've made it this far, so do we really need it?

Yes, yes, yes. Listening Out Loud is what everyone wants from everyone else. And I'm here to tell you, you can do it. Maybe even like it. Not only that, when you listen well, you get better at speaking powerfully. You become more attuned to language, energy, nuance, and impact. There is a reciprocal relationship between building your listening and your ability to express yourself—both will blossom.

Here you are, here I am. Let's crack this thing together.

The Magic Part

I am going to make you the promise that Out Loud Listening is magical. Just like Harry Potter or Merlin or Glinda the Good Witch. Am I over-promising? No.

As an Out Loud Listener you are full of experiences and creativity and playfulness. You are a precious resource in supporting your conversation partner. Not an empty canvas but a present, collaborative comrade who is creating possibility through conversation. Your colleague trusts you and you get to be on their side, you have their back. An energetic exchange occurs between you, a connection is built, learning happens. Magic.

Before I get too far ahead of myself, I'll leave this idea here for you to consider: It's not just polite to listen. That the quality of your listening affects other people in important, lasting ways. What if you attend to your friend in such a way that he feels seen, understood, relieved, encouraged? How about supporting a colleague to experience a safe space? A place she can express how interesting, smart, conflicted, funny, and deep she really is. A place where you are in it together. A place beyond the superficial, where the usually hidden is revealed.

I believe I waxed poetic right there so let me calm down. Everything I just said is still true. But you don't only use Listening Out Loud in fancy, special moments. It is an everyday, built-to-last, takes a beating, works every time, keeps on ticking, won't let you down kind of tool. For use in a 2-minute chat, a 10-minute catch-up, a 30-minute one-on-one, a 60-minute meeting, or maybe most of the time forever and ever.

The truly amazing part about Listening Out Loud is, once you get in the habit, it is so so so easy. Even fun. Because every conversation is a learning lab: you don't have to know diddly about the topic, it's really hard to do wrong, and relaxing is far more helpful than stressing.

Rightness is Overrated

One major speed bump for us to navigate, in our pursuit of fabulous listening, is the modern human addiction to being correct. I worry about even bringing this up here. It might be too soon to let this slip; that being incorrect, even wrong, is an acceptable alternative when listening.

That feels a little creepy to even write out because I'm just as devoted to being right as anyone else. Like it's a competition? Yes, exactly like a competition. What I mean here is the superiority of my opinion over yours. And, of course, yours over mine. For many of us, there's a pressure to succeed, to prove, and to show others. I win if I know better, know more, know the "truth." This is precisely what is not needed in order to listen well.

With Listening Out Loud you are engaging with your comrade—about his experience, his wonderings, his plans. So, your attention will be over there, with him. How can you know what is going on for another person? You can't. One of the reasons FOR conversation is so we can understand each other better. Talking things through is where insight, learning, and discovery happens. You are free to be curious, free to make guesses, free to get it completely wrong.

At the risk of repeating myself, your accuracy is not the point here. At first, it can feel strange to offer something in the conversation that you're not sure about. For instance, I might say to my colleague "You sound excited about this job offer." And he responds, "No, I'm terrified." Okay then. Instead of me collapsing in frustration because I got it wrong, we just go from terrified, as in "What's terrifying about this?" My being correct about his feelings is not important. Him getting to talk about his experience is. You may not believe me yet about this, which is fine. You may never believe me about this. You can still be a great listener. But this is the part that makes listening easy. I like easy.

Listening Out Loud

If you've heard of Active Listening before, some of this will be familiar. We are definitely standing on the shoulders of those who have come before us. The saintly Carl Rogers, the psychologist who believed in unconditional regard for his clients, first wrote about Active Listening in 1957. His method for connecting with his patients was resoundingly effective. What he brought to these interactions was appreciation and encouragement. Rogers was a champion for the inherent abilities and capacities in every individual.

However, by the time Active Listening got translated for the rest of us, it was diluted. When I took a quicky workshop on it, in the 1980s, we practiced looking the person in the eye, nodding, and not talking much, if at all. There was no mention of regard or esteem or concern, for the person speaking, unconditional or not. When the listeners were allowed to talk, we were to repeat the exact words the speaker had used. I might as well have been a tape recorder. Hated it.

After that, I found that even when I knew what to do, repeat back, I would not do it. For me, that meant that the other person had won somehow. If I did that, I was being weak, or I had lost the argument. And anyway, it was obvious what they said. They'd just said it! Why was I supposed to say it again?

I struggled. Because my internal operating system, my mindset, my reasoning about why it might be useful to listen this way, remained untouched. I didn't believe in it. So, while I had moments of "maybe there's something to this" I quite successfully batted those away. Active Listening had been handed to me as an answer, an opinion about what was good for me, that I had not asked for. Remember those authority issues that I have? Yep.

Carl Rogers does deserve top billing as the Godfather of Listening, but a lot has happened since 1957. In the decades since then, the study of human thriving has blossomed. We know more now than we ever have about social interaction, relationships, mindsets, adult development, emotional intelligence, happiness, and leadership. Now it's clear that when people are learning, knowing the why of a thing, the philosophy behind the doing, the beliefs underneath the actions, help us to change. Together, we'll delve into these aspects of listening.

I'm a big fan of this new knowledge about the human condition. The odd effect on me, though, of the tremendous amounts of new insight and research, is a giddy overwhelm. I want to read every book, hear every podcast, listen to every interview. This, that and the other! Then I hit a wall. It's too much, it's too hard, I'll never get it all, why bother. Melodrama anyone?

Then, I had an "Aha" moment. There are a few classic behaviors that work in human dynamics which remain constant. I don't need to read and know everything. New knowledge is certainly welcome, but I don't have to feel bombarded by the latest and greatest. The fundamental skill of Listening Out Loud is the basis for successful conversations of every kind and situation. The value of Out Loud Listening is absurdly broad.

Now that you know all that, are you ready to hear what Out Loud Listening is? Okay, here we go. Your mindset about who you are as a listener majorly matters. You get to be a willing participant and co-discoverer with your colleague / friend / partner in what they are trying to express. Your role as an Out Loud Listener means that the energy of your attention is empowering, and you are entirely focused on your conversation partner. (No checking of texts to see if someone better has come along.) You deeply understand that your Out Loud Listening is more valuable than your opinion or advice.

This mindset for listening will support and energize the behaviors, the doings, the actions, that really work. With a salute to St. Carl, yes, summarize back the content you heard. But don't stop there. Especially important, is also naming the feelings being expressed. I'm not sure this sounds quite as thrilling as it really is. But we'll get there. For this book is a detailed guide to the external skills and the internal mindsets that lead to Superstar Listening.

> "We have two ears and one tongue so that we would listen more and talk less. "
>
> –Diogenes (Greek philosopher, 412 BC-323 BC)

Concerns You Might Have

If you're not used to Listening Out Loud, it may feel uncomfortable, even weird at first. You'll be shifting your attention away from what you think and refraining from offering your opinion or advice. Which can feel destabilizing. Who am I, if not my opinions? The thing is all change feels uncomfortable, not natural, not "like" you; only because you're not good at it yet. Improvement takes effort. Which makes me want to pull the covers over my head.

But one thing I've found helps me try new things is enlisting a friend or two. I tell them, "I'm trying to get better at _____. I'd like to practice. Would you be willing to help me for the next 5 or 10 minutes?" People are often so flattered to be asked to help they're perfectly willing. And with the outside chance that they truly will be listened to, everyone says yes. Asking this way also means you don't have to do it well. It's practice, not real! If you botch it, no harm done. You'll probably just sound like you normally do. This is a low-stakes gamble if ever there was one.

The proof, though, in why it's so great to listen this way, happens when you actually do it. Because the way your conversation partner responds is what will convince you it's worth the effort. Usually, when a person feels heard, they relax. Their shoulders go down, they take a breath, they can then think more clearly and creatively. But here's another bit of magic. It doesn't just impact the speaker. Both of you will likely experience more calmness, more learning, more depth.

Admittedly, there may be people in your life where you can absolutely predict what they will say in response to you. I know that Eric, my husband, and I, years ago, had an entirely repeatable pattern. I'd come home from work and want to tell him about my day:

> I'd say, "I was in a meeting with Denise today and she lost her temper again!"

> He'd say, "You have to stop going to meetings with her!"

So. He's mad at her for upsetting me. He doesn't want me to be unhappy. To get me back to happy, he tells me what to do to fix it. I'm mad at him for telling me what to do like I'm an idiot. I can't just not go to meetings! Rather than supportive togetherness over dinner, we're arguing. Not at all what we wanted.

Later on, as we explore more about Out Loud Listening, I'll come back to this example because together we upended this dynamic. So even if these behaviors feel strange, you'll get to conduct some playful experiments.

Another worry you may have is that this will take a lot more time. I have a couple of thoughts on this. One is that some conversations are about efficiency and getting things done quickly. You don't need to Listen Out Loud in those. You absolutely get to choose where you use it and it's not appropriate all the time. Like when Indiana Jones falls in a snake pit, he needs help getting out, not a conversation about it.

Secondly, when you try listening like you're "supposed to," and give people time to talk, you probably learned not to interrupt. The tricky part is that once people feel they are being listened to, they want to continue talking. Because, finally, someone is listening. They will talk and talk and talk. And you think you're supposed to wait until they are done. Truthfully, they might never be done. So, of course, it takes too much time.

Out Loud Listening is not letting your friend talk until they run out of things to say. It is targeted, focused, and time bound. You are not a receptacle for noise but an engaged conversation partner when you are Listening Out Loud. Someone who is also aware that there is a space-time continuum that we are all subject to.

In this book, I'll give you workable ways to manage time and facilitate flow. Also, fabulous listening means you can identify misunderstandings, clarify interpretations, re-negotiate goals, all of which end up saving you time, sooner. Useful, or what?

Leading is Listening

Broadly speaking, we all have tasks to get done and people to get them done with. Relationships with these people matter. Indeed, the quality of our relationships affects the quality of what we get done. For me, I want to enjoy the people I'm working, creating, and living with. I don't mean to say that you have to befriend everyone. You do not even have to like many people. (Whew.) Even so, listening well builds a camaraderie and collaborative spirit that is precious.

This is especially true for people in leadership roles. In the early 2000s Jim Collins, a business performance researcher, was determined to find out why some companies are consistently great while other organizations that struggle to achieve mediocrity. Initially, he was adamant that the answer could not be leadership. There had to be something else going on. After reams of data and years of analysis, it turns out it is leadership that determines whether or not a company realizes great results. But not the stereotypical high-profile, big personality, I-did-it-my-way type of leader.

In his book *Good to Great*, Collins described the leaders who led the most successful organizations as Level 5 leaders. The leaders he interviewed were self-effacing, quiet, even reserved. He reports that, "They were a paradoxical blend of personal humility and professional will. They are more like Lincoln and Socrates than Patton or Caesar." Indeed, the most effective leaders connected with people throughout the company inviting them in to help, to contribute, to negate and poke holes, and to share the role of leading. What is the behavior that opens these doors? Listening Out Loud.

In my coaching work with a wide variety of leaders, I've observed that the ability to genuinely listen creates the foundation for a positive, collaborative culture. You may have heard the saying that people don't leave a company, they leave their boss. That's how much relationships matter in the workplace. They have a direct impact on an organization's ability to reach its desired outcomes and results.

From my perspective, leaders are everywhere. Whatever your job or role or title, you are a leader when you act like one. Not by bossing others around or acting like a know-it-all. Real leaders Listen Out Loud. And you know what is especially great here? The exact same Out Loud Listening skills you use as a leader will also deepen your relationships with your loved ones—children, siblings, old friends, spouses, and parents. These are the people we can forget to listen to, take for granted, or think we already know.

No doubt, it takes courage to Listen Out Loud. Yet, I know that you are up for this adventure. You'll learn so much about how to engage with others you'll likely end up a hero in the Listening Hall of Fame.

Play Date

Let's be judge-y together. Please identify someone you feel is a good listener and someone who's a terrible listener. Could be a celebrity, a public figure, or a family member, or someone you work with.

○ What do bad listeners do (or don't do) that makes them ineffective?

○ What do good listeners do that make us feel listened to?

CHAPTER 2

It's You

"People, if you pay attention, change the direction of one another's conversation constantly. It's like having a passenger in your car who suddenly grabs the steering wheel and turns you down a side street."

-Garth Stein (American author of *The Art of Racing in the Rain*, 1964–present)

Peace would surely reign across the land if people figured out how to listen to each other. However, one of humanity's amusing quirks is blaming others first. Recently, I had a participant from my class ask me, "How do you tell someone they stink at listening?"

When I say, "I want you to listen to me," what do I mean? Just what does an ideal listener do? Fortunately, because our species has wanted other people to be better listeners for so long, we've had time to pull together a list. Below, you'll find the ideal inventory of positive attributes for how to listen well. How does it stack up with what you feel makes a good or bad listener?

- Focuses on the speaker / Not distracted
- Open-minded / Not judgmental
- Curious / Asks good questions
- Includes Feelings & Non-verbals
- Accepts different perspectives / Can manage own opinions

The challenge with ideal inventories like this is that they make it look easy. Just do this—how hard could it be? But these are the be-all, end-all behaviors that are perfection achieved. It's like watching a professional athlete and thinking, "Oh, yeah, I could do that."

I took a gymnastics class in Junior High so when I watch the Olympics, I'm full of, "I remember this. Oh, I was good at the balance beam, I could totally be on this year's team." No, I really could not. Similarly, when you see the Ideal Listener list you might think, "I already do this." No, you really do not.

This Ideal Listener list only tells you what the external look of listening is. What about how to enact behaviors that will have this impact? Let's begin by rewinding the process of listening all the way back to you and your inner world.

The Me Channel

Dear reader, I appreciate you. You are here attempting to improve your listening. But we have to begin with sobering news. You are completely self-involved. So am I. This is our embodied structure at work; our survival strategy is hooked up to me, me, me. Thus, I have an automatic conversation running in my head all the time. Where my attention is on myself, the spotlight is on me. My focus is on my thoughts, my feelings, my conclusions about myself and others. The Me Channel.

Here's what mine is saying right now:

o   I wish I had some chocolate chip ice cream.
o   Why isn't Sandy returning my texts. She's a bad friend.
o   An Olympic medal is completely doable.
o   Did that guy just cut in front of me?
o   TACOS! No. Yes. No. Salad.

My brain and body are, necessarily, interested in my survival and my self-interest. As are your brain and body where your awareness / your spotlight is on you. Each of us is listening to our own inner soundtrack of opinions, ideas, judgments, wants, needs, and insecurities. I've got my own Me Channel; you've got yours.

This reminds me of a parody I once saw, of a tarot card. The original card is The Sun which is glorious. Huge, gorgeous, golden sun with rays shining in all directions. An ecstatic cherub rides an angelic horse everywhere surrounded by blooming flowers. It symbolizes new beginnings, joy, the blossoming of the earth, growth, possibility. The joke card has the same gorgeous sun but written in the middle of it in big black letters is "ME." There are small moons circulating around the sun and they are labeled, "my stuff" and "my friends." An entire solar system that has ME at the center of it.

This is how most of us listen, most of the time. Me to myself, you to yourself. It could be fun to have you tune in to your own internal voice right now. What's it saying? Maybe something like, we're really in a golden age of TV, just look at the size of my gut, where's the dog, this book is genius....

For simplicity's sake, let's call this Me Channel, Level 1 Listening. This is the internal monologue, the voice that you can hear inside your head all the time. I am making fun of Level 1, a little bit, but elements of it are incredibly important. We humans are wired to make sense of what's happening around us. What does this mean to me? What do I think about this? What's in it for me? What should I do next? This quick-wittedness of ours is a superpower.

Level 1 is how we navigate the world. It's where we interpret language and meaning, to figure things out for ourselves. If your officemate says, "There is smoke coming out of our trashcan" you'd immediately realize the rejection letter you were burning earlier was still smoldering. Then based on that understanding, Level 1 helps you figure out what to do next. If this had ever happened to me, which it hasn't, I would silently pour my coffee over the smoking remains and go outside for a scream.

However, when it comes to listening to a compatriot, elements of Level 1 are terribly limiting. Our conversation partner is trying to express her experience, her thoughts to us. But Level 1 means we are listening to ourselves, our interpretation, our opinions about what she's saying. Not what she is truly trying to communicate to us.

Right here, I'd like some dramatic music to play, with the big timpani drums—bom bom BOM! This was huge news to me. My Level 1 is mine alone? Not everyone else thinks the way I do? But I'm so right about what I think. Am I right? I'm right.

Habits that Block Listening

There are predictable ways that we humans do not listen well to each other. They stem from our Level 1 focus; the world is based on how I see it and my certainty that I see it accurately. Internally, in ignorant bliss, I know what's appropriate and I know the way things ought to be done. If someone's not doing them that way, they're doing it wrong.

I should back up a bit: our brains are just trying to keep us alive. Admittedly, an important and necessary foundation for listening, is to be a breathing, living creature. Yet the quality of said life is a nuance the older parts of the brain do not care about. The priority is just, not dead. There's a scene in *The Last of the Mohicans* where Hawkeye is holding tight to his lady love, while a waterfall crashes and booms around them. Just before he jumps off the cliff, Hawkeye shouts to Cora, "Stay alive, no matter what occurs!" That's what our brains are saying to us, without any of that romance or excitement.

Whether I feel joy, fulfillment, or contribution—meh, not so important. Thus, from its primaeval perspective the brain tries to scare me. Frequently. If anything is new, different, or surprising— be suspicious. It might bite. This worried, defensive point of view is an unconscious automatic setting for most humans. And when it comes to listening, this fear-based warning system is what we pay attention to. We listen to the part of the brain that prioritizes our safety. And we listen, take the messages to heart, and repeat them when we try to listen to others.

Our built-in cautiousness is important and useful. But we go overboard with fear, doubt, worry. What if they don't like me? What if I'm not smart enough? What if they see through me? Avoid failure, criticism, disapproval, stupidity, weirdness, weakness. For thousands of years, in many traditions around the world, we have chronicled this fear-based voice. There are different names for it—monkey mind, inner critic, saboteur, devil on the shoulder, gremlin. They tend to run the show without our noticing, whispering threats that we will lose our place, be voted off the island, disappeared. These internal voices sound perfectly sane and accurate. Their job is to keep you where you are because you haven't died yet. And to make sure everyone you care about is similarly cautioned to not change a thing.

There's one particular voice in our heads that I'd like to call out—The Judge. We ask real-life courtroom judges to evaluate evidence, to discern truth from lies, and to make good decisions about difficult topics. This ability to assess and differentiate from a logical point of view is a powerful tool that every one of us needs.

The Judge that I'm talking about, though, is an exceedingly critical and disapproving character. Mean and shaming. We have expectations for how life should go and are often assessing, in our heads, if it is going as it "should." These "should" messages usually grow out of inherited values and standards from parents, culture, school, religion, movies, and social media.

The most common message we receive is some version "You Are Not _____ Enough." Fill in the blank with "smart" or "thin" or "strong" or "educated" or "quiet" or "attractive" or "disciplined." Really just don't get your hopes up.

When I was writing my first book, here's what I said to myself,

> You should write faster; what a waste of time.
> You should be more interesting; no one will read this.
> You should be original; this has already been done.
> You should be smarter; this is stupid.
> You should stop.

To some of you that might just sound like reasonable advice. That's what I thought at the time, "That's my realistic side." But no, that's the JUDGE trying to scare me away from what I really wanted to do. Better safe than sorry remember? Don't do anything new. You might get killed.

I was used to hearing that voice in my head. I interpreted it as pragmatic counsel. I mistakenly thought that voice was how to get moving, shame myself into action. It did not work. Actually, it's a terrible way to be spoken to.

For our purposes, listening to our own internal Judge voice is the first way that we block our own listening to another person. We hear that Judge and offer up what it says.

> My niece says, "I'd like to go to UCLA film school."
> And I say, "You'll end up living in a dumpster!!"

I judged her idea as bad and wrong. Then follow up with my superior idea.

> "My advice to you is to get into air conditioning. With climate change, that industry's gonna take off."

I offer up my Level 1 worries, concerns, and judgements. Thinking I'm being helpful! I am not being helpful. I am not meeting her where she is. I'm trying to make her come to where I am, which is by the way, according to my Judge, the right, correct, appropriate place to be. And, after all, the safe one.

Quite often, the first way that we react to others is with our Judge. I say react because we're not really listening. Listening Out Loud is quite different. But first, a quick review of the Human Condition and reactive habits.

More Automatic Reactions (That Are Not Listening)

From the point of view of being a human animal, life is terrifying. Most days we're just hoping not to be kicked out of the campground and eaten by the lurking hyenas. Given this motivational backdrop, we have predictable ways that we respond to other people. We try to look good, be cool, act smart. All in an attempt to prove to ourselves, and to others, that we are worthy of something, anything. Most humans engage in a version of these tactics; see which ones fit for you.

Got This Under Control

> This kind of looking good is not joyful self-assurance. The fear instinct, which wants to avoid looking bad, is in charge. So, I'm going to pretend confidence, I got it figured out, I understand, I'm the decider, I'll explain, I'm in control. Even if I'm just acting that way in order not to be seen through. How I am coming across is more important than listening.

Please Be Pleased

Agreeable people are just lovely. My husband is one of these amiable types and often wonders aloud, "Can't we all just get along?" I love that—his warm heart wishing for peace. (It saddens me, just a little, to tell him it'll never happen.)

Strangely, it is possible to be too agreeable. There's this odd version of people-pleasing that doesn't work for listening. From this place, whatever the topic, I'm going to agree, say "yes, you're so right," smooth over feelings—don't want to disturb anything. Mostly I want my conversation partner not to dislike me, so I'll apologize for lots of stuff, blame myself and others, and hope she sees what a nice, inoffensive person I am.

Already Knowing

When the movie *Titanic* was released in 1997, I asked my mom if she wanted to go see it. "I don't think so," she said. "I know how it turns out." Is it bad I thought that was hilarious?

Being in the know is considered a sign of intelligence and status. To prove myself, show I'm good enough, I need to not be surprised, not be ignorant. Because I already know. You can see how this closes me off to listening.

As my colleague is talking, I'm thinking: "I've been there, I've done that, I'm way ahead of you. I don't need to hear your words because, really, I already know what you're going to say. You can stop talking now. It's my turn. Your mind is so simple! I can read it without you even speaking."

(There's also "I've Done Everything You've Done, Only Better" Listening.

You tell me, "I went to Italy last summer."
And I respond, "I bought a whole town in Italy. For a dollar."

You tell me, "I've got to get my knee worked on."

I respond, "My entire leg is pretty much bionic now.")

Winning

This is a big one; probably the enormous umbrella under which all these habits live. Current neuroscience research is finding that "being right" is an emotional state. We like that winning feeling. In the sense of winning an argument, a point, a trivia contest. I'm right and you're not.

My brother-in-law, Jay, is a lawyer. I once asked him what he thought about mediation. I wondered if all kinds of people should learn mediation strategies so lawsuits would be less frequent.

His wife, Dee said, "There aren't enough lawyers to help people anyway!"

Jay jumped in, "You gotta be kidding; there are way too many lawyers!"

Dee says, "Oh yeah? How many?"

Jay says, "That have passed the bar? Or not passed bar? In California? Or in the nation?"

Off they went looking up on their phones, as fast as their fingers would take them, to find these numbers and continue the contest. Meanwhile, I poured another margarita wondering about mediation.

In this information overload age, it can be seductive to fact-check instead of remaining in a conversation; to win by proving wrong.

These are common ways that we react to each other in conversation. They should not be mistaken for listening. Rather, these reactions, habits, default settings result in our colleague, friend, or sibling not feeling heard. When the Me Channel is in the director's chair these are the scenes we produce.

From a hero's point of view, on the journey toward championship listening, this list of habits is a little confronting. There's a classic saying about admitting you have a problem is the beginning of a solution. That's where we are right now. I hope you see that this is a necessary pain-in-the-ass learning moment for progress to be made. Isn't self-awareness fun?

Play Date

A couple of observational exercises for you, where you get points for telling on yourself.

- For a week, observe, gently (but not too gently), how your Judge, Pleaser, or Know-it-All jumps into conversations. Check in on how often you reacted rather than listened.

- Choose two people in your life that you'd like to improve your listening with. (I request that at least one of them NOT be the most, vile intractable person you know. There needs to be some chance that you might actually be able to practice with this specimen, so pick on the nicer end of the scale.) For now, simply mull over how you usually interact with these two—see what patterns you might notice. Your patterns, to be precise, not theirs.

CHAPTER 3

In Your Head

"Adventure is not outside man;
it is within."

-George Eliot aka Mary Ann Evans
(English novelist, 1819-1880)

Why do I listen and respond the way I do to other people? My behavior is often prompted without me even being there. What I mean is, I'm listening at Level 1 to the ME Channel. I've got default rules that can just run on automatic; I can react in my habitual ways without much thought.

Like walking on a treadmill, I'm staying in the same place, not falling off but not really moving forward either. Or even like a bird attacking its own reflection in a window. There's a survival instinct running the situation that is not working out too well. Or, the classic example, a vinyl record when the needle is caught in a groove. Where that skip is, those notes just keep playing again and again.

Similarly, in conversation, we fall into predictable grooves. The dilemma is, even if we are not happy with the results of our behaviors, we keep acting the same way. What we have here is a failure to communicate. The brain is not thinking things through itself. As in this quote from Carl Jung, the Swiss psychiatrist: "Until you make the unconscious conscious, it will direct your life and you will call it fate."

The short version of the situation is this: My thoughts, in my head, have me behave in a way that makes sense to me. (You have this too.) The trap, though, is we are not aware of the thoughts that are running our behaviors. They just feel like the way it is and we don't examine why we act, say, and do the things we do.

So, our actions make sense, and nothing need change. Even if we don't like the results we're getting. What was that? Yes, even if we don't like the outcomes our actions are creating, let's keep acting that way only louder, or faster, or sooner. Then they should work. (I may have already mentioned: the definition of insanity is doing the same thing over and over again hoping for different results.)

In the previous chapter, we investigated a few common ways that we try to win in this life; pleasing, controlling, knowing. On the face of it, these are terrifically useful ways to be. Get stuff done, make people happy, have good ideas. Yet in the realm of listening, they lead to one common reaction in conversation. Let the scales fall from our eyes...

Fix It Now

Doesn't offering advice on how to fix a problem sound like a noble thing to do? It makes sense that if I've listened well than I can go to the next step and give you my ideas. When I first became a coach, I would ask compound, complex questions that were a suggestion in disguise. "Don't you think, that if you re-wrote your resume and used a new font but didn't tell your husband you were applying for the job, that you'd have a better chance?" No way no how does this qualify as good listening.

In my years of teaching people how to listen well, offering advice is absolutely the hardest habit to change. How come? My thought is that we spend so many years in school, where a single right answer wins us praise. Later on, we are often hired to be an expert in a particular content area, and we prove our value with knowledgeable answers. As a parent, rearing a child involves a lot of correcting, advising, directing. The result? We get brainwashed into thinking offering advice and expertise is what conversation is. And this automatic "provide-a-fix" reaction can become a one-response-fits-all-situations. In every discussion, we are to give others either a correct answer, a solution, or our opinion. How I "add value" is by informing, analyzing, frowning. Quickly too. There's no time really. Let's be efficient, jump to the answer so we're done.

Say my friend tells me that she's worried about her eyesight. Whether I want to please her, look smart to her, or feel useful to her, I can get all of that done with, "You should drink carrot juice." The glaring problem is that this has turned in to me listening to myself and my thoughts about what she is saying. My judgment, my idea, my knowledge. Not even subtly, the conversation has turned to be about me, not about her.

This is why our results are often frustrating. On my side, I'm like, "I gave her by best answer—why is she not excited? Ingrate." On her side she's wishing I'd actually listened to her concerns, her experience, her story. Sigh.

> "Yeah? Well, you know, that's just, like, uh, your opinion, man."
>
> —-"The Dude" played by Jeff Bridges
> in *The Big Lebowski*, 1998

Mindset for Listening Out Loud

Initially, when I tried to get better at listening, I did not realize that my mindset mattered at all. I wasn't aware that I had internal rules, like a software program, that ran automatically for how I was to respond to people. This unconscious internal program was based on me proving myself. Looking like I knew what I was talking about, that I was fun to be around, and nice enough.

So, my focus, when listening, was on me and how I was performing. But I wasn't aware that these behaviors were being run by an internal program or mindset. Just felt like, this is what listening is. I've got nothing else to go by.

I had a desire for deeper, better conversations, I didn't have different mindsets to try on, a new internal software to help guide my conversations. I could tell what I was doing wasn't working very well and doing more of the same did not help. I would try the behaviors of Active Listening, but I was still in the show-I-know mindset. Give short, fix-it answers. While I could learn the "How to Do" listening behaviors, when I'd try them my entire being felt vulnerable. Not a feeling I liked. This discomfort always won.

You remember that robot who appeared on the vintage TV show *Lost in Space*? This was way back when, but when danger lurked, he would yell out to the hero of the show, "Danger, Danger, Will Robinson!" And his superior smarts would save the day. Whenever I tried to listen actively, I'd hear a similar shout inside me: "Warning, Warning, Basic Humanoid! You must add value or be cast out!" Thus, I'd stray back to opinions and defending my ideas and every other sort of not listening.

Fortunately, there are a couple mindsets to support Superhero Listening. I wish I'd found them a lot sooner. They took some searching for. Almost as if the secret sauce must remain a secret? Or is only for specialists? Let's change that, please.

These mindsets were pivotal for me. They allowed me to have an attitude toward my conversation partner that I chose, was consciously aware of. I wasn't running on autopilot anymore. What is it that I need to think, inside myself, in order to behave in a way that has my friend feel listened to? What is a mindset that will move me away from automatically giving my opinion? What could I listen for in my colleague's conversation to better understand him?

I'm starting to sound kind of artsy fartsy. Well, we are venturing into a bit of philosophy so maybe it's warranted. These next few ideas are for you to play with as thought experiments toward Listening Out Loud. Meaning you get to try on a belief, act as if it's true, and see how it affects your behavior.

This ought to feel playful and experimental, even celebratory. Not a "Resistance is futile" assimilation by the Borg approach. Pain and suffering will not improve your listening. More along the lines of light, easy, and Mr. Rogers' invitation "Won't you be my neighbor?"

Smarter Than That

Let's look at two places we can create new mindsets with which to approach listening. The first is your beliefs about your conversation partner. As we've seen, our typical reaction is to help with a Level 1 suggestion or opinion. This kind of implies they are a dummy. As a general rule, it does not lead to better conversation.

Shocking idea #1. Your conversation partner is creative, resourceful, and has plenty of smarts to call on to solve his own issues. You may already be arguing with this idea. I know I did. I was reared in a culture, as you may have been, that wasn't terribly encouraging in this regard. Schools tend to focus on grading us on a competitive scale about who's smart, who's dumb, and who's dumber. Thus, status based on intelligence is deeply embedded in our lives. While I enjoyed learning, as most people do, school can warp how much we trust our own and other people's abilities.

A similar unempowering impact can happen in other parts of our cultures. Particularly, where an external authority makes the rules. The religion I was raised in claims, from birth, I'm a corrupt sinner. Can't be trusted without serious policies and procedures for what to do and what not to do. While religions include lessons on kindness and compassion they're often enforced unkindly.

We live in a world with institutions that are meant to help us. Yet they usually rely on obedience and fear of punishment for them to work. If this is the background against which we learn to communicate with each other, of course we listen poorly. I'll just give you the advice I've been told, and you give me the advice you've been told.

Between individual people, though, there is room for much more. Shocking idea #2. Every one of us has an inner world which, I contend, is even larger than the outer world. We humans are generous, loving, and brave. Nuanced, subtle, and perceptive. There are heroes everywhere paying it forward, backward, and in every direction.

Popular culture doesn't advertise this much though. A grim view of human nature as selfish and evil, with only a thin veneer of civilization painted over it, is threaded through our history. This is the dominant story we tell and are told, directed by our own bias toward negative news. But current research, which highlights more positive perspectives about what humans are "really" like, is gaining ground.

In the 2019 book, *Humankind: A Hopeful History*, Rutger Bregman offers a telling example. Have you heard of *The Lord of the Flies*? A global blockbuster since its publication in the 1950s, the novel is by the British writer William Golding. After the horror of WWII, he imagined a story of English school boys who, when shipwrecked on an island, regress into murderous, blood-soaked enemies.

When Bregman first read the book as a teenager, he didn't question the truth of the message. But as an adult he lost faith in the idea that humans are born depraved. He hoped to directly rebut Golding, by finding a real-life example of shipwrecked children to see what would truly happen. He found one.

In June of 1965, six boys living in Tonga, near New Zealand, decided to skip school. They found a boat, and with a few provisions, took off. Terribly lost, they drifted for 8 days but then landed on a tough rock of an island. Over a year later they were rescued. What had happened to them during that time? Had they become monsters of selfishness and violence? Not quite. They had created a small commune. A food garden, rainwater catchment in hollowed out tree trunks, a makeshift gym and badminton court, and a permanent fire were elements of the life they made together.

How had they managed? They'd cooperated, collaborated, and cared for each other. Jointly, they designed a calendar, to work in teams of two, on the garden, kitchen, and guard duty. Sometimes, they did quarrel. Their agreement was that each of the arguers went to opposite ends of the island to cool off. When ready, they'd apologize and regroup. After their rescue, the boys remained friends for the rest of their lives.

There's more to this incredible story. But this small slice of it reveals a fuller picture of humanity, far more compelling and generous than *Lord of the Flies*. Indeed, the author, Golding, had a profoundly dark view of the world. He was a troubled man, prone to depression and alcoholism. While he was a talented writer and teacher, Golding felt he identified with the Nazi's motivations and impulses. From that "sad self-knowledge" of innate savagery, he wrote his despairing novel.

Did I just go too far off the deep end there? I think so. Part of my point, part of the fun here, which may not sound like much fun, is that you get to examine your own ideas about humanity as a whole. Because we're marinated in so many dystopian, nihilistic narratives, I must remind myself to choose a fuller, more complete, appreciative view of my fellow human beings. Particularly for fabulous listening. Your mindset about the person across from you matters.

For now, imagine someone in your life, that's only mildly irritating to you. Not a doozy of a jerk just yet. We have to work up to that. Let's play with the perspective that this conversation partner of yours knows more than you think and has plenty of insight and understanding of her own. Like a game of make-believe. Try this belief on, like a new jacket, just for two minutes. What happens inside you when that could be true? I hope it has you feel a bit of relief and ease.

Admittedly, it took me a while to get to that point. I was so acculturated to judging everyone, along with myself, as deficient I found it a hard habit to break. As the idea made headway through my immune system, here's what I got:

- I do not have to fix a thing—she has the answers inside.
- I am not responsible for this—she is the owner of her choices.
- I do not know her life the way she does—she can figure this out in a way that works for her.

While these ideas are meant liberate you to listen, rather than "fix," you might wonder, "If I'm not doing those things than what AM I doing here! What else is there?"

We'll investigate that very question in the rest of this book. Right now, my hope is that the pressure for you to remedy a situation or have an answer can just melt away like the ice in a gin and tonic. The bottom line is they (your co-worker, spouse, employee, family member, boss, friend) are qualified to live their life. Once you learn that lesson, you can partner with them in living it well.

Standing Shoulder to Shoulder

Have you heard the phrase "Tunnel Vision"? Literally, it's a physical problem with the eye, where you can only see properly what is in the center of the field of view. Metaphorically, people who rigidly focus on a single goal or point of view are said to have Tunnel Vision.

When I'm coming from Level 1 Listening, it's a kind of like Tunnel Vision. The Me Channel is narrowly focused on my opinions, my likes & dislikes, what I want, what I think is important. Kind of a Tunnel Channel Vision. Each of us is ultra-talented here with that self-focused voice always talking.

When I want to Listen Out Loud, I have to switch channels because my colleague's Channel Vision is more important than mine. It's time to dial in on what she is interested in, what's weighty for her, what she's feeling, and what she sees is next.

The mindset here is I am on her side, not on my side. I am here for her, not for myself. I am standing shoulder to shoulder with her looking at life, not arguing across a table. I am beside her as an ally, a champion, a co-investigator, a partner, a challenger, a coach, focused on her and her experience.

This may sound silly but here's a wordplay for you. Your being present, with your full attention over on your colleague, is like giving them a gift or a present. Your presence is a present—a happy-making surprise.

Corny, perhaps. But it's a way to think about it: "Let me offer my attentiveness to this person so that they feel seen, heard, validated." All those things that people feel when they are paid attention to. My presence is a present! And guess what, giving presents feels almost as good as getting them.

After I have Listened Out Loud to another person, I'm usually in a better mood. I feel as if my listening mattered. We made some progress. Got an insight. Learned something new. I was there for my fellow human. I gave them something of my consideration and my support. Frankly I'm proud of myself that I listened well.

The Inside Job

Who knew that listening is based on our internal mindset? To change how I responded to others I had to start there. I hadn't known how calcified I was in certain ways of responding. Changing my mind is what allowed me to change my listening. When I consciously decided that my friend / colleague / relative had plenty of experience and smarts, I could relax into my job of exploring that with them. When I got to be curious rather than analytical, I even liked people better. They didn't seem as frustrating and pig-headed as they used to. My mindset shift led to different conversations than I'd been capable of before. And as I evolved, my relationships did too.

This tuning up of my internal mindset allowed me to implement the outward, behavioral skills of Listening Out Loud. Truly, these two interweave together, supporting each other as you go. As a hero, on a journey of growth, some days the behaviors may feel easier for you. Other days, the mindset. Perfectly normal. Simply move forward with what you have. Experiment, play, and allow for pleasant surprises.

Play Date

Research on how to implement new habits recommends short, frequent forays that are easy and happifying. Delightful!

The new habit to try on is relaxed attentiveness. (Meaning—NO FIX NEEDED.) You're still paying attention but are under no pressure to advise or hurry. This exercise is internal to you so you can begin to feel what it's like to listen from this mindset. That's what to consider just now, your experience of releasing having to have an answer.

To make this easy, you could choose a regular time to practice and then reward/celebrate yourself afterward (also a terrific help in creating new habits). Say, 10 minutes of practice at 10 am for 10 days. Each minute of practice earns you a superiority dance of 10 seconds. If you go for all ten minutes, that means an all-out boogie down for 100 seconds to your favorite tune. Rock on.

If you feel comfortable enough, try this mindset with one or both of your two people. Maybe you speak, maybe not. It matters more that you're noticing and adjusting your internal habits.

CHAPTER 4

Me Channel on Loudspeaker

"Most people do not listen with the intent to understand; they listen with the intent to reply."

-Stephen R. Covey (American self-help author, 1932-2012)

What does the Me Channel sound like in conversation? We are so used to hearing it from others and speaking from it ourselves, we can entirely fail to spot it. So, here's an example for us that illustrates the common stereotype of how we "listen" to each other. In this exercise I've asked three colleagues to listen to me from Level 1. They have complete permission to be self-focused, Me Channel Listeners. You'll see that I tell them about a real issue in my work life and then they each respond from their Level 1. (In a later section, we'll compare this to how Level 2 Listeners responded.)

Lauren:

I'm an executive coach and work with individuals on their leadership and impact. I also do a lot of culture work inside organizations. Helping them collaborate, share power, create learning cultures. Good stuff.

Some recent coaching clients are with private equity companies who also own and run smaller companies. The equity people are brutal.

They're really hard on themselves. They are also tough on the small companies. You know, make the numbers, no matter what.

I'm coaching people and see these dynamics that are difficult for them to work in. But all I can do is work with the individual. I don't seem to be able to intervene in the larger system. I'm helping people make it day to day. But the bigger picture is really complicated.

Okay—let's hear your Level 1!

Kerry L.

It just felt like you were leaning really heavily into emotion and, like, your feelings. This seems like a business problem that needs to be approached with more of a logical point of view. I would start there honestly.

(Level 1: Judged emotions, gave advice)

Jonas T.

I know some people exactly like that! They seem very similar to these former friends of mine Pete and Terry. I'm not sure you should be working with these people.

(Level 1: The listener's own experience, gave advice)

Miranda O.

I kind of missed some part in the middle there, but I mean, I think you should work with them the way they want to be worked with. That's probably what should happen.

(Level 1: Distracted, gave advice)

Lauren:

Thank you so much for NOT listening! What I got from you three was, stop your whining, here's a fix, go do this. You performed Level 1 Listening perfectly.

You can see the three people listening to me are trying, offering help, doing what they can. But the impact of their listening is limited. It's from their point of view, from their concerns, and from the voice of their Judges. Not really about me, but them.

This is when they, you, me—many a hero considering an adventure—says, now wait just a minute. What else is there for me to do? Isn't offering my opinion and telling what I know, listening? I so believed this. Not consciously. I didn't know this is what I thought. But it was under there.

From this unconscious place, too often, my version of listening was to talk about what I'd read most recently. That way, it wasn't my idea for a fix, but a smarty-pants, qualified, author's idea. It had to be better than what my friend and I could come up with. Regrettably, this simply ends up as another serving of Level 1 Listening with a dollop of look-how-well-read-I-am.

Me, Myself, & I Channel

Back in the 1990s, when Forgiveness was getting a lot of press, trending even, in the self-improvement world, I did my reading. One story was about a Viet Nam POW who was still mad at the Viet Cong for holding him as a prisoner. I certainly understood that. But the wise person forgiveness expert said to him, "You're still in prison" if you cannot forgive them and yourself. Oooooh. This war veteran then took on the work of forgiveness so he could be free. A young woman in the Peace Corps, volunteering in a destitute part of the world, was killed. Her mother forgave the two men who murdered her and enlisted them in the work her daughter had so loved. These were terrible, riveting, wonderful stories.

I was sold.

One Sunday afternoon, I headed from our house in downtown Austin to visit my parents in their Northwest Hills home. We'd lived in that pile of yellow bricks for years and years. I sat in my usual place at the kitchen table and mom was in hers. Dad was away teaching a formation flying class, so it was just the two of us. Which, truth be told, was how we liked it. Now we could talk about anything and everything without having to make sense or finish a thought or come to a conclusion.

But she seemed edgy, irritable.

"Are you mad at me?" I asked.

"No, no. I haven't been sleeping."

If your mattress wasn't so hard..." I said.

"I need to tell you something I haven't told you before," she said.

"Oh no," I moaned.

"Years ago, when my parents died, there was a small inheritance. Equally divided between the six of us—my brothers and sister and I got $2000 apiece."

"Okay. That's not so bad."

"My brother Sean, your uncle, asked each of us if he could borrow our $2000 so he could start a business. No one would loan it to him. Even your father told me not to. But he was my little brother, my favorite."

"Mom, you know that guy's a jackass."

"But he needed help, and I could give it to him. So, I did."

"You what? You gave him your money?"

"Yes. We agreed I'd loan it to him for a percentage of the business. I wanted to invest in him."

"His business is huge. I didn't know you owned any of that."

"Right. That's because he says I don't."

"See, jackass."

"I still can't believe it. He says he'd never have given me part of the business. 'That'd make me a prisoner,' he said. I keep going over and over it."

"Oh mom. There's no point really is there? It was decades ago. Everyone else was right about him."

She nodded slowly. Turning away, to look out the window, she continued, "Now he has disowned me. Tells me I'm no longer his sister. He won't speak to me..."

"Oh darn. That's a real loss," I smirked.

Time for the hammer.

"You just have to let it go, Mom! You know, Forgiveness. You're being held captive by this thing. There's nothing you can do about it. You have freedom in your own hands."

After a pause I asked, "How about some chips and salsa?"

The Great Unlearning

This conversation was pretty typical for me, and my family. Opinionated, snarky; it was fun—to feel superior and smart and sassy. But in this case, I completely missed out: on my mother, her experience, and really supporting her. When I think back to that conversation, I am regretful, sad. I loved my mother, and felt we were friends, buddies even. But I don't see that in this exchange. She was trying to confide in me, and you see how I left her by herself?

I'd bet that you, too, have had conversations that you wish had gone a different way. You are completely capable of creating better discussions if you're willing to observe yourself in action. Good news, you are already improving. Bad news, continued study of self is required. Thus, it's useful to minutely review what I, and you, do, say, and think while in these talks that go sideways. Then I will have a chance at recognizing my habits as they happen. Which then gives me more choices on how I want to engage.

So, why don't we examine my Level 1 Listening in excruciating, embarrassing detail, yes? Let's use my epic fail as an example. For I had habits to unlearn and move past. You, on your heroic path, will also have listening habits that are not worthy of you. Time to get out the magnifying glass.

"Are you mad at me?" I asked.
[Level 1, it's about me for I am the universe's center]

If your mattress wasn't so hard..." I said.
[Level 1, my correct opinion on the superiority of pillow-tops]

"Oh no," I moaned.

[Level 1, focused on my discomfort as I like to stay happy]

"Okay. That's not so bad."

[Level 1, my feelings of relief that I get to stay happy]

"Mom, you know that guy's a jackass."

[Level 1, my very right, correct, obvious opinion]

"You what? You gave him your money?"

[Level 1, my judgmental outrage about what could have been mine]

"His business is huge. I didn't know you owned any of that."

[Level 1, my less judgmental opinion as I wonder how much it's worth]

"See, jackass."

[Level 1, notice how very right I am please]

"Oh mom. There's no point really is there? It was decades ago. Everyone else was right about him."

[Level 1, judgment: this is boring]

"Oh darn. That's a real loss," I smirked.

[Level 1, judgment: the less of him the better]

"You just have to let it go, Mom! You know, Forgiveness. You're being held captive by this thing. There's nothing you can do about it. You have freedom in your own hands."

[Level 1, I know how to fix this and also you are to blame]

"How about some chips and salsa?"

[Level 1, I'm hungry so let's change the subject]

Well, that was gross. My self-oriented habits kept me stuck inside these kinds of reactions. I'm afraid that's true for many of us humans. My default response, when I realized what I'd done in this conversation, would be to let my internal Judge yell at me. Bad daughter, bad, bad, bad. But you know what? Shame and guilt aren't great motivators for change. I've also noticed that once I've felt miserable enough, I let any corrective action go. Don't have to change because I suffered already.

Therefore, a little self-compassion, self-kindness is just the ticket here. On this heroic journey of life, there's an underlying possibility in every moment. To move beyond myself, to engage with another person, to offer my attention as a witness, as a balm. It's generous. It improves the mood, the energy, the day. But there is no "have to." The choice is ours to make.

What I want for us is to have listening skills so that we get to choose. If you don't know how to listen well, you can't do it. But once you know, you can decide, this is what I want and who I am, right now. Having a Level 1 based conversation is how most interactions go. Feeling bad about that is just a major waste of time. Better to feel inspired to connect a bit more, experiment, play, to see what happens when you do.

Play Date

While each of us is a sparkling diamond of intelligence and wit, there are places in life where we can't be bothered. We just go on automatic; we fall into a role or habitual pattern that is how we usually are.

With the two people you've chosen to concentrate on for these exercises, consider how you interact with each one of them.

○ How are you predictable with them? What is your go-to response?

○ How much does your Level 1 Listening steer the conversation?

CHAPTER 5

Getting Loopy

"I know that you believe you understand what you think I said, but I'm not sure you realize that what you heard is not what I meant."

–Robert McCloskey (American author of *Make Way for Duckling*, 1922–1996)

Currently, I'm coaching with a finance executive who is on top of the world. Literally in one of those expensive new office towers in Manhattan, high floor. Jeremy has proven he's a star, a genius, a winner. Money, accolades, triumphs galore.

But his boss, his colleagues, his clients, all have a complaint about him. He never stops multi-tasking. He cannot or will not remain focused on the person in front of him. No matter the importance or status of his conversation partner, he is checking texts, glancing at emails, looking at papers on his desk, waving at passersby in the hall.

This has had a huge impact on how people view him. They feel disrespected. They react like Glen Close's character in *Fatal Attraction*—"I'm not going to be ignored!" Yes, Jeremy's smart, talented, and entertaining. But can he be trusted? If he can't attend to a person right in front of him, what does that say?

I asked him what makes it hard to focus on others. Jeremy feels that he's missing out, something else might be happening. He wants to stay stimulated, up to date. So, the work is to shift his energy to being curious about the person in front of him. To be sparked and informed by them, rather than something outside the conversation.

It may well be that an incoming text is far more interesting than who you're in conversation with. Not the point. There are tangible effects that listening has on the people around us. This is where feelings of respect, trust, reliability, fairness, connectedness are created. This is why listening effectively is so miraculous—it has an impact on people's state of being. And you can create that. On this hero's journey you can use your powers for good. Or you can keep swiping.

Focused Attention

Let's face it, we have far too much information competing, dominating and pushing for our attention. The temptation to multi-task has never been greater. You might even pull it off sometimes. But the research shows that when interacting with another person, a divided attention span is, by definition, inattention. People can tell if you're not with them. And they don't like it.

A few years ago, I was on the phone with a woman I'd hired to be a mentor coach for me. I'm in a bad mood, pouring my heart out, hoping for some support. I can hear, through my headset, the sound of keystrokes on a keyboard.

"Are you typing?" I ask.

I am miffed. Here she is writing an email or shopping online or....

"I'm taking notes on what you're saying," she replies.

Then she reads my words back to me.

My bad. Yet that experience pierced me a little. Before she explained, I was hurt, even embarrassed, that someone important to me thought I wouldn't notice her disinterest.

One of the fundamental elements for effective listening is managing our own attention. This is bad news. Never has there been a better time for distraction, entertainment, or busy work. Netflix. eBay. Tinder. Wordle. All easier than having to interact with another human in real time.

Let me hurriedly remind you, why Listening Out Loud is a worthwhile skill to pursue, even if it's harder than choosing what to watch on movie night. Long before electricity, what we had was each other. Conversation was threaded throughout our days and nights. While cooking, playing games, building, teaching, making music, storytelling, caring for children, dancing. With our family and tribe, for tens of thousands of years, this was the good life.

Nothing's really changed about that. What has been proven to help people live long, happy lives? Social connections, enjoyable relationships. The quality of the life we live is based on the conversations we have. You are taking hold of the relevance, the richness, the depth of your experience in this lifetime, by Listening Out Loud. Is that enough to pull you off Candy Crush? Tough choices, I know.

The truth is that your concentration, your focus, your attentiveness are vital ingredients for fantastic listening. And for Level 2 Listening, these qualities are foundational. It's time to concentrate on your conversation partner and tune into their Channel.

When I was a manager in a big tech firm, I interviewed a sharp young woman, Layla, for a job and hired her. Months later she told me what impressed her the most during our interview is that when my phone rang, I didn't look at it nor answer it. That was it? How about my fine intellect, my cool outfit, my general awesomeness? Layla made me realize the power of making the person I'm speaking with, the center of attention.

You might even imagine a bubble around you and the speaker. The two of you are in the most important interaction on earth right now. Shine your focus and attention on them. You don't have to stare at them like the Cookie Monster would a Fig Newton. But energetically, that level of interest is helpful; the focus is on this other person, their experiences. Not yours so much.

The way our brains evolved, we humans benefit from looping information, knowledge, ideas that move from inside our own heads, to outside of us. Our brains do not work like a linear, logical computer crunching its way to an answer. We are designed to interact in order to learn and change. Rather than keeping my thoughts in my brain,

I'll share my idea with a friend, see what he does with it in his head. When he passes it back to me, it's changed, altered, improved. Then I have this new information to respond to which creates the next loop between us.

At first, I pictured each of us, my friend and I, with a yo-yo. I'd toss mine out in a circle toward him. He'd pitch his to me with a twist. But then I realized I have to release what I'm saying. Let it be his for a while. Same when he returns my thoughts to me. We can't hold onto them but must allow them to move through the other person. This is an energetic exchange looping between us, morphing and shifting as we go.

That's when I got a new idea, which to me, was lovely. The loop between us, as I listen to you and you listen to me, is a version of the infinity symbol. Representing, as it does, a timeless, boundless space for what's possible including creativity, emotions, and connection. The actual symbol for infinity is a ribbon folding across itself in a recurring stream. The easiest way to describe it is the number 8, on its side. See how it's almost like an Escher print where you can't tell where it begins or where it ends. Just like how we communicate with each other.

That day I had a call with my encouraging, positive friend Jeff. I told him about my fantastic idea.

He said, "Lauren, that is so over-used. I thought you'd have something really special."

"Bye," I said.

Other images that I tried to bend to my will were spirals, photosynthesis, boomerangs, potlucks, and Ponzi schemes. But what is it that captures a swinging, flowing, alternating dynamic? I couldn't find it. They say, when taking exams and playing at improv, go with your first thought. While I'm terrible at both exams and improv, it was my first idea and it's pretty. That's good enough criteria for me.

Unlike *Toy Story's* Buzz Lightyear, though, we're not traveling to "Infinity and Beyond!" We're traveling toward each other. So, how about calling it an Affinity Loop? Affinity is about connection, liking, similarities, common ground, harmony, and accord. We swap energy and words with each other to create rapport, bonds, and even growth. Very cool.

> "It is not from ourselves that we learn to be better than we are."
>
> –Wendell Berry (American ecologist & author, 1934–present)

Level 2 Listening

The word "listening" also refers to sound waves entering your ear—one of the five classic senses. As if that were all there is to listening. Actually, the interior structure of our ears, tiny porcelain puzzles that dance, is extraordinary. For our purposes, though, passive receiving of sound is not enough. If you're sitting there, expressionless, staring into space, your conversation partner may lose confidence that they are speaking to anyone but themselves. To listen is a verb. Active, engaged, focused, thought-provoking.

How can you demonstrate you're listening? You respond! After listening to your Very Important Person, your job is to represent back to them both the content and emotion they've expressed. The two elements to pay attention to in Level 2 Listening are words and feelings. I'm going to split them up right now in order to distinguish these two parts. We'll put them back together once we've defined them.

Level 2-A. Words / Content

The first part is what the other person's words mean, the content of what they are saying. You're listening so well, that you'd be able to tell them what they said. Sounds obvious. It is. I'm afraid it feels so obvious we rarely do it.

I was coaching a high-powered manager, recently, whose direct reports complain about his arrogance and the challenges of working for him. I explained Level 2 Listening as a tool he could use to connect with people and bring more of a coach approach.

He smiled and said, "You mean where, like a dumbass, I parrot back the crap they just said?"

Aha, I thought, I remember that feeling.

I laughed and said, "Right? Like they can't remember it or something? But, yes, that's exactly what I mean. For you to act like a dumbass."

Luckily, he laughed. So, I had a chance to further explain the difference between Level 1 and Level 2. And also pick apart this less-than-helpful idea of "parroting." Officially, and let me say it loud and clear, there are no parrots in Listening Out Loud. Even though they are astoundingly intelligent and all-around magnificent creatures, we're on our own here, in human interaction territory.

Here are some official descriptions for the skills that show that you are listening.

- **Paraphrase:** Restating or rewording, to give the meaning in another form.
- **Clarify:** To make an idea or statement clear; to free from ambiguity.
- **Reflect Back:** To cast back (light, heat, sound) from a surface. To give back or show an image of; mirror.
- **Summarize:** Previous statements are compiled in a concise review; recapitulation / "recap."

Each of these words is a slight distinction on what and/or how you're saying your response. I'm not so worried about the differences between these for you right now. Use one, use them all, use a favorite, mix and match. Each one of them works. They all offer similar assurances that you are listening carefully and are engaged in what your conversation partner is saying. I'll go into more detail later, but this is an important skillset when it comes to listening like a superstar.

For a quick example of each of these I'll use a quote from Mark Twain and see how I fair. Twain was an American writer during the 1800s who wrote funny stories based on his travels and boyhood adventures. His most popular books were *Tom Sawyer* and *Huckleberry Finn*. I adore his style and here's a bit of his advice on writing.

"An average English word is four letters and a half. By hard, honest labor I've dug all the large words out of my vocabulary and shaved it down till the average is three and a half... I never write metropolis for seven cents, because I can get the same money for city. I never write policeman, because I can get the same price for cop.... I never write valetudinarian at all, for not even hunger and wretchedness can humble me to the point where I will do a word like that for seven cents; I wouldn't do it for fifteen."

Now for my attempts to show I was listening:

o   My **Paraphrase** to Twain: So, you've worked hard to get rid of long fancy words in your writing because short words do the job just as well.

o   My **Clarifying** with Twain: The principle here is that if you're paid by the word, pick short easy ones?

o   My **Reflecting Back** to Twain: Sounds like you feel multi-syllabic words are pretentious, maybe even a version of showing off. Simple words are more accessible for a wide readership.

o My **Summary** for Twain: Big words bad.

One more way of giving back to your conversation partner is to **Articulate What's Going On**. This is where you make an observation about what you already know about him and what he is saying now. You succinctly describe what you see happening without judgment or the need to be right. You're offering up a perspective for him to consider.

o "I know that creativity is important to you. This new position sounds like you'll get to use it more often."

o "Your long-term plan has been to develop your own business yet the details of it seem to be weighing you down."

o "You are such a hard worker, but you are surprised by success and compliments."

Listening and then **Articulating What's Going On** has a particularly powerful impact on your partner in conversation. Not only are you focused on them in this moment, but you're also bringing in what you know about them from your past together. You've attended to them so well that you can connect the dots between who you know them to be and what is happening now. I just got goosebumps. This kind of appreciative listening is a magic art.

Level 2-B : Mood / Energy

The second part of Level 2 Listening is noticing the mood or energy of the person speaking. You might wonder why this is important—I already got the story from their words. Well, human beings are complex. We usually have feelings about what we are saying. I'll use one sentence to show you what I mean...

I say, with a smiling face and high energy tone of voice, "I got the promotion."

You could say, "Sounds exciting!"

I say, with a blank face and dull tone of voice, "I got the promotion."

You could say, "You sound disappointed."

I say, with a sneering face and sarcastic tone, "I got the promotion."

You could say, "You seem underwhelmed."

This part of Level 2 Listening is a Special Spice. You are showing your colleague that you are attending to him so closely that you can tell how he's feeling. Superb. And important, because research shows that a good amount of communication is transmitted through mood and energy. The exact percentage is difficult to pinpoint but between 50-70% of communication is not about the content of the words. If you're not tuned into this aspect of listening, you may miss quite a bit of the plotline.

Feeling Impaired

Emotional states may be less obvious to you at first. Your own and other people's. Many of us are raised, me included, to ignore feelings and act like everything is fine. The idea seems to be, let's pretend we're machines, and wow, we will save a bunch of time. Don't bring your emotions to work. Don't be overly dramatic. Don't be nosy. Maybe this way we'll hardly have to converse.

Un-repressing, un-ignoring, un-doing this enculturation takes time. Some parts of the hero's journey are lifelong experiments. If this element of Level 2 Listening seems challenging, not a problem. Because once you get the feel for naming an emotion, you'll see how easy it can be. When you start looking for them, they appear.

Here's an example. I have a colleague, Noah, a consultant, who was telling me about a new project he landed. He described how big the company was, how well-known the brand, how large the project, and how high-profile it would be. On the face of it, sounded like a terrific win for him. Yet Noah's tone of voice was monotone, flat.

If I were coming from Level 1, I'd ignore that and say, "You are so lucky." But no. Being a rocking good listener, I said, "Sounds like you won a real opportunity but are feeling ambivalent about it now…"

Noah responded by describing how he felt discouraged. Layers of bureaucracy were being put between him and the people he wanted to work with. In our conversation, Noah realized he was trying to be a good soldier and go along with what he thought the company wanted.

My part was noticing his words and energy. I tuned into Noah's Channel—what he was really saying, what he was feeling. I supported him in discovering what was going on for him. Through our quick chat, he saw more clearly the path to take. Noah went back to the organization and renegotiated how it would work best for him. Turns out that's what they'd wanted too but they didn't know how to bring it up.

For many of us, the extent of our emotional vocabulary sounds like Mongo from *Blazing Saddles*, who had the IQ of sea algae: "I good." "I not good." I heard an actor in an interview recently describe the emotions he learned growing up—anger and sarcasm. Fortunately for all of us, there are more than that.

Psychologists call them The Big Five:

- Mad
- Bad
- Sad
- Glad
- Anxious

These are a great place to start. Later on, we'll explore emotional nuances, if you like that sort of thing (which I totally do) but this list has us ready to roll.

Listening Out Loud in Action

Here's a re-run for you. A couple chapters back, I shared an example where I spoke to a small group about a work challenge. A few of them listened from Level 1 and the others from Level 2. You've already read what the Level 1 folk had to say. Now we get to compare those to the responses from the Level 2 listeners.

Lauren:

I'm an executive coach and work with individuals on their leadership and impact. I also do a lot of culture work inside organizations. Helping them collaborate, share power, create learning cultures. Good stuff.

Some recent coaching clients are with private equity companies who also own and run smaller companies. The equity people are brutal. They're really hard on themselves. They are also tough on the small companies. You know, make the numbers, no matter what.

I'm coaching people and see these dynamics that are difficult for any of them to work in. But all I can do is work with the individual. I don't seem to be able to intervene in the larger system. I'm helping people make it day to day. But the bigger picture is really complicated.

Level 2 Listeners:

Patrice C.

I could tell from the words you were using and your expressions how frustrating this experience is. And it sounds like you are really trying to help them long term. But it feels like you're not able to make as much impact.

(Level 2: Summarized content & named emotion)

Jason B.

I sense that you're discouraged. You're coaching these executives, but it doesn't lead to that bigger culture change that needs to happen. So, it feels like, man, I'm doing my best, but there's only so much I can affect.

(Level 2: Named emotion, Paraphrased content)

Marianne O:

I know how much you value helping people shift or change the limiting situations they're in. Feels like a level of powerlessness for you.

(Level 2: Articulated What's Going On, named emotion)

Lauren:

Brilliant! Yes. You each captured my experience. I feel understood by you all. I even calmed down a bit. So helpful.

Do Over

I certainly have a multitude of conversations in my life that I wish had gone differently. The one I told you, with my mom about her brother? That one is near the top of the list. As a do-over, I'm going to cross out what I originally said. Then add in a Level 2 version of what I'd aspire to say knowing what I know now.

She seemed edgy, irritable.

~~"Are you mad at me?" I asked.~~
"You seem unhappy. What's up?"

"No, no. I haven't been sleeping."

~~"If your mattress wasn't so hard..." I said.~~
"That is so hard!"

"I need to tell you something I haven't told you before," she said.

~~"Oh no," I moaned.~~
"Alright. I'm ready."

"Years ago, when my parents died, there was a small inheritance. Equally divided between the six of us—my brothers and sister and I got $2000 apiece."

~~"Okay. That's not so bad."~~
"Sounds like a fair division."

"My brother Sean, your uncle, asked each of us if he could borrow our $2000 so he could start a business. No one would loan it to him. Even your father told me not to. But he was my little brother, my favorite."

~~"Mom, you know that guy's a jackass."~~
"You really loved him."

"But he needed help, and I could give it to him. So, I did."

~~"You what? You gave him your money?"~~
"Wow. You supported him when no one else would."

"Yes. We agreed I'd loan it to him for a percentage of the business. I wanted to invest in him."

~~"His business is huge. I didn't know you owned any of that."~~
"That's my mom! Savvy investor. How does it feel to own part of that empire?"

"Right. That's because he says I don't."

~~"See, jackass."~~

"Wait a second, let me catch up. You, out of all your family, invested in him and now he is saying you didn't?"

"I still can't believe it. He says he'd never have given me part of the business. 'That'd make me a prisoner,' he said. I keep going over and over it."

~~"Oh mom. There's no point really is there? It was decades ago. Everyone else was right about him."~~
"Oh no. This must feel like such a betrayal."

She nodded slowly. Turning away, to look out the window, she continued, "Now he has disowned me. Tells me I'm no longer his sister. He won't speak to me."

~~"Oh darn. That's a real loss," I smirked.~~
~~Time for the hammer.~~
"This goes from bad to worse, mom. It's as if he's turned on you, to be cutting you out of his life like this. No wonder you're not sleeping."

~~"You just have to let it go, Mom! You know, Forgiveness. You're being held captive by this thing. There's nothing you can do about it. You have freedom in your own hands."~~
After a pause, I asked, "How about some chips and salsa? And we can talk about what would support you right now."

This version of the conversation stars an open-minded listener; one whose agenda is to have her mother feel heard and cared for. I regret back then I was not being capable of overriding my automatic smart-aleck-ness. If I'd had this conversation with her, what impact would it have had on our relationship?

Do you have a conversation, when you think back on it, you wish you could change? And wonder what might have happened if you'd listened well? My hope is that you don't beat yourself up about it. But instead imagine a future possibility. That next time, you'll be ready for a more connected, in-this-moment conversation. After all, the trials and tribulations of the hero's journey are the preparatory steps, the training needed, for the more important and powerful experiences to come.

Play Date

A fun approach to practice Level 2 is in a low-stakes way. I like to slow this way down and write down my response. This gives me time: to shift from Level 1, to focus on the speaker, to consider what I think they said, how I'd like to say what I heard... See how many steps there are?!

○ Start with movies and TV—after a character says a few lines, pause the show. What would you say back from Level 2?

○ Rewrite a conversation that didn't turn out well, using your newfound Level 2 listening skills. After rewriting it, on the page or in your head, notice how you feel.

CHAPTER 6

Not Invisible

"I'm always relieved when someone is delivering a eulogy and I realize I'm listening to it."

-George Carlin (American comedian, 1937-2008)

In my attempts to decipher the motivations of human beings, I've developed a few pet theories to explain some of our odd behavior. One is the Peek-a-Boo Syndrome. Like the game we play with babies. See me? Can't see me. What I mean by that is, sometimes, I think I'm invisible and nobody notices me and anything I do doesn't matter. I stare at strangers or twirl my new skirt or pull up my bra strap and no one sees.

The other side of Peek-a-Boo is I think everyone is watching me. Probably as I make a fool of myself. I'd better look pleasant and smile, just in case. Or, depending on the situation, look tough. Look cool. Smart. Someone could be filming. Like that movie with Jim Carey, *The Truman Show*, where his entire life is beamed out to millions of people each day. That could be me!

I swing wildly between these two different ends of the spectrum. No one can see me or everyone's staring. This is a totally self-oriented Level 1 ME channel experience. So, here I am judging myself: I'm great, I'm terrible, I'm an idiot, I am brilliant. I'm also judging everyone else the same way. I'm better at this than he is—ha-ha! She's better at that than I am—oh no!

Blah blah blah & more blah blah blah.

When we stay in Level 1, we're judging both ourselves and other people. My brain will busy me with worry, fret, envy and convince me this is worthy territory. Then comes the neato trick of extrapolating that since I judge my own stuff, I'll also judge my friend's stuff.

The ability to pay close attention to others get atrophied because of our internal focus. What is happening right in front of us, in the moment, gets overlaid with stuff about ourselves. People are actually communicating so much, all the time, but we have forgotten how to interact with it or them.

I myself am a terrific example of unconsciousness. For many years I knew that what I felt, and thought was completely obvious and, also, the correct way to think and feel. Because of this, I did not notice that how I spoke, what I said, the look on my face, and my tone of voice affected other people.

Here's an example. A while back, I was working inside a large tech firm and was in a morning meeting with some colleagues who knew me well. I was tired, with that sand in the eyes feeling, staying quiet, drinking espresso. My stretch goal for the day was not to lay my head down on the conference table.

A few minutes into the meeting one of them asked me, "Are you okay with this?"

I said, "Yeah."

"You don't seem okay."

"It's good."

"Well, why aren't you saying anything?"

"Because it's fine. I don't have much to say."

"Are you sure?"

"I'm FINE!" I shouted.

I thought I'd hidden myself, but they could see me. They were trying to check in with me yet in a sort of blaming way. This is one of those ridiculous messes. Without realizing it, I was communicating in many ways my low energy and desire to be left alone. They were responding to my non-verbal cues and interpreting what those meant, incorrectly. With our communication lines broken, we got mad at each other. Isn't this just a fine how-do-you-do that happens far too often between folks?

Confusion reigns. In this example, I think I can hide, be invisible. I am seen when I don't want to be. But how I am seen by others is their "why," their explanation for my behaviors. Not what's true for me. The result is a negative experience for me and them. Ironically, they tried to include me, which is what I usually want, and I bit them on the hand. From my side, I tried to tell the truth, politely, so they'd move on. But they were pushy. Neither of us was seen, heard , or understood by the other the way we hoped to be.

We humans are neither invisible nor unseen, but we are not always visible or seen in the way that we want. If we don't listen well, but rather I count on my interpretation of you and you count on your story about me, we block connection from happening. Most of us want to be deeply understood and validated which is the result of Listening Out Loud. Belonging, being included, is such a profound human need. Attending to non-verbals is a powerful means to reaching a validating end.

There is much to see and hear and sense from the person you are listening to. Especially when you tune your full antennae onto them. Let's investigate what you can pay attention to that you might have been ignoring until now.

Non-Verbals and More

What we're talking about here is noticing the energy and mood of the person who is speaking. What does that mean you can look for? Non-verbals.

I have to tell you I get irritated by words that are non-something else. Like non-fiction, like non-entity, like non-verbal. I want these things not to be non-. If you are a Not-That, then what are you? I want them to have an identity, to have their own word. Do I have that word? No.

However, in my coaching work I use the model developed by the Co-Active Institute. There we use the term "geography." The word geography refers to the study of the physical features of the earth and its' atmosphere. In the coaching or conversational context, "geography" means the physical observable elements of the person you're listening to posture, gestures, facial expression, amount of eye contact, and tone of voice.

The idea is that people often express what they really mean, plainly for us to see and hear, if only we pay attention. The clues are all around us. Surprisingly, words are not always as important as we think. Really listening often goes beyond words; we could call it Full Body Listening.

Posture

First let's look at posture. It can be as overt as your friend with his head in his hands vs. he's pacing the room. The different physicality gives us some clues to what he might be feeling. Head in hands might be defeat or sorrow. Pacing could be excited tension.

Our physical posture, our movement, is linked to how we feel. A quick little demonstration here with your own posture. Please slump your shoulders forward, let your head droop, gaze downward. After a few moments in this position, what do you feel?

The second part of the experiment is, from this position, to get excited. Fill yourself up with joyful, happy, and enthusiastic energy!

I'll admit that was a little trick. It's very likely that when I asked you to get excited, your head came up, your shoulders went back, and you started to smile. Of course, you did. Our physicality is connected to how we feel! Like a puppeteer, our thoughts and emotions pull on the strings that move our bodies and facial expressions around. Thus, if you pay attention to the geography—the observable physical elements of a person—you get lots of clues. Which is a major ingredient to fantastic listening.

The insight is this: Someone's physicality (their posture, their physical position, their gestures) is hinting to you what they are feeling. The way people hold themselves, the tension or relaxation of their body, the direction they are looking, all may be related to their internal landscape. Noticing a person's physicality helps you tune into them and their experience.

Voices

Another element in a person's geography is their voice. Consider the notions of having a voice, voicing concerns, speaking up, singing the praises, or saying what you mean. Voice is how we make ourselves known in the world. The voice, which literally is how the air in our lungs passes through our facial bone structure, is deeply affected by our moods, our physicality, our psychology.

As an Out Loud Listener, attending to the sounds of the voice can add insight and depth to your conversation. Noticing a monotone speaking style vs. an expressive style can lead to new awareness. Pace and volume: Is the speaker's voice soft and slow? If so, what might that indicate about their mood? If the speaker's voice is loud and sharp, what might be occurring for them?

Perhaps your colleague began a conversation with a quick energetic pace but when you ask about his new boss, his pace slows and is more deliberative. What happened there?

Voices are like the soundtrack for a movie. The music helps you know what's going on. Cellos can hold sadness, brass bands are triumphant, quick violins are for Psychos. Similarly, the sounds of our voices convey messages to attentive listeners.

Faces

The saying goes that the eyes are the window to the soul; I say the face is a set of French Doors. We have 42 facial muscles that are incredibly talented. The range of their capabilities is vast. They can radiate big overt feelings, slip subtle messages, or repress internal storms. As a listener, you're actually looking at your friend's face to discern the unspoken messages there.

Years ago, I visited the family of a young boy who was struggling with the social aspects of school as he was mildly autistic. This was before smart phones but on their kitchen fridge was a worksheet with several "emoji" faces on it. His homework was to look at each emoji and take a guess at the emotion it was expressing. I've since wondered, optimistically I admit, if the everyday usage of emojis has helped us get better at readings emotions in real people.

Three examples for you to play with:

Human Face	Emoji	What emotion is it?

What I see with our, now common, use of emojis is how blatantly powerful the face is in communication. Even a flat cartoon with scant eyebrows can send a valuable update on an emotional state. Not only that, but we can bypass language altogether. Around the globe, an image of a face conveys more than 1000 words describing it.

Imagine the impact of observing and engaging with, not an image but the look on your conversation partner's face, live, here, now, in the moment. Some beyond words magic can happen here. You are able to see what he cannot, his face. You can offer him news from the front, what it looks like from your view. You may even fathom more about his feelings than he himself had previously realized.

Noticing vs. Knowing

The pioneer researcher on facial expressions is named Paul Ekman. Starting in the 1960s he observed and cataloged different peoples' emotional experience along with their associated facial expression. In his book, *Emotions Revealed* he describes how across cultures the same facial expressions are related to the same emotions. Humans are deeply connected in how our bodies process feelings.

Ekman went on to further fame when he studied micro-expressions, tiny movements of the muscles in the face that are reflections of how we are feeling. Not only do these rapid expressions show emotions, but they can also reveal when the speaker is lying.

In fact, there was a great fictional TV show around 2010 based on his research called *Lie To Me*. The actor Tim Roth starred as a professor who knew all about the physical "tells" that revealed people's emotions and often enough whether people were lying or not.

In one episode a young woman disappears but her mother doesn't seem too broken up about it. She was saying all the right things, but her face was devoid of concern. I was convinced that she was behind her daughter's death. A few minutes later, we find out she was a heavy user of Botox. Her facial muscles were purposely deadened so as not to cause wrinkles. She was grieving for her daughter, just not visibly. I felt a bit bad about my rush to judgment there.

This story holds an important lesson. Posture, facial expression, and body movement all hint at what is going on for the person with whom we're talking. But it is only a hint, subject to different explanations and all kinds of variables. What we have is an informed guess. A guess, which is often useful, but that isn't always going to be right.

Where we can get into trouble is believing we've interpreted our friend correctly and that we know why they are acting the way they are. That's probably our Level 1 Listening talking. We're projecting our notions onto someone else, making up a story. That's why I don't really recommend books or articles that promise to tell you what non-verbals mean. There's no way to know for sure as this is not a literal science.

For instance, it's a popular idea that people whose arms are crossed are closed off and are disapproving. I for one, love crossing my arms. It's comfortable and even helps me relax as it pulls my shoulders down. What are some other reasons I might cross my arms? Maybe I have a spot on my blouse I'm trying to cover. Maybe I have indigestion. Maybe I'm showing off my fancy rings.

The best bet is to assume we don't know. What's so great here is you don't have to know. As an Out Loud Listener, we are making guesses to engage, prompt, and encourage our conversation partner. In the next section, I'm going to show you how to turn noticing into a powerful tool for engaging and encouraging your conversational partner. For now, it's enough to tune in and start paying attention to the priceless information emanating from every person around you.

Play Date

This is your chance to wake up your ability to notice what is happening in front of you, in the moment. To get started, you might turn off the volume for a TV show. Watch one character for a few minutes and see what guesses you can make.

I'll confess to being a people-watcher. In a public place, choose a person to observe and see what clues you get. Ultimately, you'll get to use these observational skills in conversations with your colleagues and friends. Right now, you're warming up your powers of attention.

CHAPTER 7

I Was Too Listening!

"Listening is a magnetic and strange thing, a creative force. The friends who listen to us are the ones we move toward. When we are listened to, it creates us, makes us unfold and expand."

-Karl A. Menninger
(U.S. Psychiatrist, 1893-1990)

Did you know there's such a thing as a Shakespeare Nerd? There are a surprising number of us; maybe you're one too. We're a fun bunch. A couple of summers ago, Eric and I wandered the U.S. to attend as many Shakespeare Festivals as we could. All over the country, in both indoor and outdoor theaters the Bard's stories are on offer. We ranged from coast to coast to see Hamlets and Pucks and Juliets aplenty.

In one charming city, in the Great Lakes region, we had high hopes for the local Shakespeare company. They'd been around for years and looked creative and energetic. Eric and I joked that ice-bucket winters must concentrate the mind toward playing outside in the summer. Thus, their zesty productions. We were also considering this town for a permanent move. If there was enough artsy culture, good restaurants, and friendly folk, we'd be hitching up the U-Haul.

On a warm June evening, the sun low in the sky, we took our seats for "Macbeth." The story is about a brave Scottish general who receives a supernatural prophecy that he will become the King. This prediction infects his mind so terribly that he and his wife plot and then murder King Duncan while he is visiting their home. Macbeth does become King of Scotland, but the guilt and paranoia of his actions drive him to tyranny and his wife to madness. A dark and bloody lesson about ambition and the pursuit of power.

As the play began, three witches took to the stage reciting the famous lines, "Double, double toil and trouble; / Fire burn and cauldron bubble'." The oldest one was maybe 12. My stereotype of witches, that I am sticking with, is that they are old. I harumphed to myself.

Macbeth was better. Beautifully, his voice rang out across the park. He had the rare ability to speak the lines and have them make sense to a modern ear. He did resemble Marty Feldman, who played the servant Igor in *Young Frankenstein*. But you know, who's to say? Unfortunately, during his best soliloquies there were "extras" coming and going on the stage, one of whom had clunky shoes. I ended up trying to figure out who was making all the noise rather than following the plot. I harumphed some more.

Lady Macbeth is always a tightrope—Mourning mother? Beloved wife? Crazy murderous bee-atch? This Lady M was a yeller. In outdoor theatre, nuance can be hard to come by. In her effort to be heard, this actress didn't do much acting. She was just bonkers from the word go. Harumph.

Finally, the intermission arrived.

"Well, that was uneven," I said.

In a low growl Eric said, "It was appalling."

I was taken aback. I'm usually the snippy critic and Eric is the generous, give-'em-a-break champion of these productions.

"But they..." I began.

"Did you hear that woman LAUGH when the king was stabbed?" Eric whispered.

"Maybe she doesn't know the story?" I countered.

]"And the murderers. That murder scene looked they were in a disco, some kind of line dance," he hissed.

"The costumes are pretty cool," I said.

He peered at me.

I defended myself with "And the setting is beautiful."

"Yes, yes, okay. The trees here are very nice." he said. "I'd still like to leave."

"Really? You don't want to see if it gets any better?"

"It will not get any better," he said.

So, we skipped out. With a weird, disagreeable tension between us on the ride home. In the morning, we chatted about where our travels would take us next. Then Eric said quietly, "There was not one good actor in that show."

For some reason, this got through to me. I didn't necessarily agree but a bell went off in my head—ding ding ding. I had not LISTENED to him. I've only told him what I think.

"Oh, you sound so disappointed by that."

He sighed. "I am. Their past productions were good. I wanted to be a fan. This is a big enough place. There should be plenty of talented people."

"You had high hopes for their shows. And even the town. It has such a creative reputation."

"Right. Maybe I was expecting too much. Such a letdown."

"When Shakespeare's bad, it can be really bad."

He laughed. "Well, we came to check it out," he said. "Now I know."

"Yeah, we're learning. Which places we want to come back to and which we don't."

"This is a don't."

"I am writing that down," I said. And I did.

Reflecting Back

What I eventually did with Eric was simple. Instead of presenting my point of view, I showed him that I understood his. Now, it's officially your turn to do this with your conversation partners. Here you are: you have a focused mindset, you are paying attention to the words that person is saying, and to their energy & their mood and facial expressions. The next step is the Out Loud part; to reflect back what you've observed.

The reason I like the "reflecting back" phrase is the metaphor of holding up a mirror for the speaker. Most of us find it difficult to tell what we look like if we don't have a mirror to reflect back what it sees. Humans also struggle with clearly knowing what we think or feel until someone else can show us a version of it.

Here's another possible metaphor for you. We often call a colleague who is a good listener a "sounding board." Meaning that this is an individual you can trust, to talk through things with—they understand you, they tell you what they see, you can "bounce things off of them."

The derivation of that phrase, "sounding board" comes from a literal physical wooden board. Before we had microphones and amplification, people who made speeches for a living, preachers, politicians, professors, would usually stand on a stage or pulpit to pronounce their pronouncements. The sounding board was a literal structure set up over or behind them to make their voices sound more distinct and to carry farther.

You as a good listener, as a sounding board or mirror, help your conversation partner hear and see what they themselves are expressing. Nifty, yes?

A couple of concerns you may have. One is, this sounds easy and obvious, to the point of embarrassing. It can't really be necessary, you may think. Yes, certainly, you don't have to reflect back every single sentence. Other than that, though, it works so well you won't even believe it. As a champion listener, you are like the magician who can pull a coin from behind an audience member's ear. Delight, surprise, look what we found!

If you feel you've tried to do this before and it didn't work, it may be that you were coming from Level 1 Listening. Maybe you were too opinionated or a bit judgmental? That just doesn't help at all. Level 2 is the way to go.

Lastly, you do not have to like what the other person is saying, and you do not have to agree with what the other person is saying. This can be challenging for us mere mortals. Much of what folks say aloud are the views that they hold. Which, naturally, are the right ones which anyone with a brain could see.

However, your role as an Out Loud Listener is simply to verbalize what you are hearing—offering back a restatement, a translation, a summary. Your Level 1 opinion does not come into this just yet. You're temporarily suspending your views and you are not saying you agree or approve. You are simply reflecting back as does a clean, clear mirror.

How to Say It

What I've found most helpful in reflecting back is knowing how to start off. Sure, I can understand what someone is saying. But to turn it around and offer it up to them begins to feel complicated. Once I got a few sentence starters, it became easier. First, I want to give you these partial phrases so you're ready to roll. Then I'll offer some examples of how to use them.

Reflecting Back Starter Phrases:

- "It sounds like you…"
- "I get the sense that…"
- "It seems that…"
- "Let me see if I've got it, you…"
- "It feels like…"

Given the challenge of having a live conversation through this written medium, I'll use some theatrical characters to practice with.

From *Frankie and Johnny in the Clair de Lune* by Terrence McNally.

Frankie: "The only time I saw the sun come up with a guy was my senior prom. His name was Johnny Di Corso but everyone called him Skunk. He was a head shorter than me and wasn't much to look at but nobody else had asked me. It was him or else. I was dreading it. But guess what? That boy could dance! You should have seen us. We were the stars of the prom. We did the Lindy, the Mambo, the Twist. All the fast dances. Everybody's mouth was down to here. Afterwards we went out to the lake to watch the sun come up. He told me he was going to be on *American Bandstand* one day. I wonder if he ever made it."

Lauren: "It feels like a great surprise that the guy who seemed like a loser turned out to be such fun."

From *The Coast of Utopia: Shipwreck* by Tom Stoppard.

Belinsky: "I'm sick of Utopias. I'm tired of hearing about them. Do you know what I like to do best when I'm at home? Watching them build the railway station in Saint Petersburg. My heart lifts to see the tracks going down. In a year or two, friends and family, lovers, letters, will be speeding to Moscow and back. Life will be altered. The poetry of practical gesture."

Lauren: "Sounds like seeing actual physical progress is more exciting than abstract ideas."

From *The Importance of Being Earnest* by Oscar Wilde.

Lady Bracknell: "I must say, Algernon, that I think it is high time that Mr. Bunbury made up his mind whether he was going to live or to die. This shilly-shallying with the question is absurd. Nor do I in any way approve of the modern sympathy with invalids. I consider it morbid. Illness of any kind is hardly a thing to be encouraged in others. Health is the primary duty of life. I am always telling that to your poor uncle, but he never seems to take much notice…"

Lauren: "Let me see if I understand—for you, a person's ill health can be a burden for others and avoiding that sounds important."

What's fun about this exercise to me is that theater is about competing interests, conflict, and drama. When I get to intervene with my stupendous listening skills, we can all calm down and actually hear the character. This is what Listening Out Loud will give you too. Reduced drama, increased understanding.

Impact on the Speaker

Weirdly, people do not listen to themselves. They want you to do that. And when you do really listen, they will think you're a genius. Something essential happens when people feel like you "got" it. There's an energetic exchange with Listening Out Loud that provides some relief and connection between the two of you.

To listen well is to figure out what's on an individual's mind and demonstrate that you take enough of an interest to want to know. We all want to be understood as a person with thoughts, emotions, and intentions that are unique and valuable and deserving of attention.

Remember a few sections back when I told you about when I'd come home from work and try to tell my husband Eric about my colleague Denise? And he'd tell me to stop going to meetings with her? He was trying to fix it for me, but we just got frustrated with each other.

Here's how we changed that dynamic. I told Eric about reflecting back. Luckily for me, he likes it when I am happy and his Listening

Out Loud made me very, very happy. When he would say back what he'd heard me say, I could relax, I felt understood.

Lauren: "Denise totally blew it today!"

Eric: "Tell me everything!" (Which made me laugh because neither of us really want to talk about this.)

Lauren: "Denise and I are in a meeting with a customer. He wants to know what training his employees have attended. She says, 'We can't tell you that.'"

Eric: "Not a great response?"

Lauren: "Denise is telling the client, to his face, that we're idiots."

Eric: "How so?"

Lauren: "Even though we *can* figure out who has taken what, it'll take a lot of admin work. The database we use is terrible, we can't trust the info in it. But she made us look bad!"

Eric: "You'd rather she'd focused on what you all could do rather than jump to what you couldn't."

Lauren: "Yes! Her immediate 'no' caught me off guard. Then I got mad. She'd answered for the whole team. I didn't want to contradict her in front of the client. But I also wanted to give him what he needed."

Eric: "You were in a bind. A 'Denise Dilemma'."

Lauren: "Right! That's exactly what they feel like. Maybe I'll name this cocktail after her."

Listening Out Loud is about the experience of being experienced. It's when someone takes an interest in who you are and what you are doing. As a good listener that's what Eric offered to me in that conversation.

I'd like to go even further here. I used to think that other people were either born interesting and fun or they were not. It had nothing to do with me—it was on them. But here's a radical idea. When I start to interact with people as if they are interesting, they become more interesting. By how I relate to them, I influence them.

Think about a time when you were trying to tell a story to someone who was obviously uninterested; maybe she was sighing, or her eyes were roaming the room. What happened to you then? Maybe your pacing faltered, or you left out details, or spoke too loudly, or you even overshared to regain her attention. Eventually, you probably trailed off while she nodded absently. You also dislike that person now, yeah? She forced you to be a bungling storyteller!

To create good conversation, give the gift of your attention and care. To listen magnificently is to be interested, and the result is more compelling conversations. The goal is to leave an exchange having learned something. You already know about you. You don't know about the person with whom you are speaking or what you can learn from them. Focus there and you will both appreciate the other more for it.

Bringing In Creativity

Here's the wild part! You do not have to get it "right." I know we've talked about this before, but with such a staggering idea, you may not have believed me then. I'm going to repeat it. Every single thing you say in Listening Out Loud can be off base, not right, incorrect.

Being right is just not the point. If you are truly attempting to understand and are reflecting back what you are getting, that is what's important. You and your compatriot are discovering what matters, as you speak, together. This is where the idea of co-creation can be helpful. You, as a remarkable listener, are offering up ideas, thoughts, observations based on what you've heard your friend say. You throw it out there, give them something to respond to, so they can think more deeply, have new insights. You're helping them talk it out.

Mostly people rattle off words, sentences, paragraphs not really believing anyone is paying much attention. So, they may not be exact, or say what they mean, or even know what they think because they've never gotten that far before. You are not trying to pin them down, like a lawyer extracting rehearsed testimony. More like you are cooking together. Each of you adds an ingredient, takes a taste, and considers what will work next.

On a subliminal level, I hope I'm influencing you with my metaphors. When you want to help your conversation partner, a metaphor is preposterously powerful. The right brain, where emotions live, is also the imaginative, artistic, visual side. Pictures in our heads speak to us more deeply than words do.

Bringing your creativity into the conversation is the playful assignment here. You see a connection, a comparison between what your colleague is saying and a symbol for it. To someone complaining about restrictive school requirements you could say, "It sounds like you're in prison..." Or to someone who›s is working hard but feels no progress, "You're busy in the beehive but there›s no honey..."

Metaphors perk people up; they want to consider this new way of looking. Occasionally, it's the perfect image and the conversation gallops ahead with it. Remember how you don't have to be right though? What usually happens is people say, "No it's not that. It's more like this..." and then name a metaphor that is more accurate for them.

"It's not a prison, it's more like a hurricane is coming."

"Not a beehive—I'm on a bus."

If I were listening from Level 1, I might say, "It is too like a beehive. You said everything is buzzing around you..." But because I'm listening Level 2, I ditch my idea because mine doesn't matter. Instead, I grab my colleague's idea and say, "Tell me more about the bus."

Sometimes your partner makes it easy for you and uses a metaphor that you can pick up and offer back. Early in my coaching learning, I had an associate who told me, "I feel the need to write a letter of goodbye, but I can't get myself to do it. I keep putting it off. I mean I feel like I'm going to a funeral."

And I said, "Well the letter doesn't have to be long..."

You see what I did there? Missed the funeral completely which would have been an easy win in the listening game. I tried to get her to write the letter. In other words, to DO something. My Level 1 fix prevented me from recognizing what she was saying. If I had picked it up from Level 2, I'd have said, "Seems like something is ending here, even dying off." That would have been Listening Out Loud.

Listening Out Loud is not about me. It's not about you. It's about the person we're in conversation with. How I, and you, add value is to offer back a distillation, a version of their experience for them to consider. This opens up the conversation, rather than shutting it down. When I say, "Well the letter doesn't have to be long…" it simply puts a burden on the speaker to act, write a letter. Or to argue, "I don't want to write a short letter, it has to be a long one." You can see where that will get us. But when I say, "Seems like something is ending here, even dying off," there are so many possibilities. They may respond, "It does feel like something is dying off, and I realize I'm hesitant to let go." See? New insight.

You and I are wildly important in our contributions here, not for our judgmental minds but for our creative selves.

Play Date

In the next three conversations you are in, bring in a metaphor. It doesn't have to be even close to the right one. That leaves a lot of room to play. You could even choose one ahead of time. What I mean is, you can cheat. Have a metaphor planned the whole time.

My secret metaphor weapon is squirrels. "You're like a squirrel storing nuts for the winter." "I see a squirrel trying to cross the road." "This sounds like a squirrel on a highwire."

Maybe you pick your favorite animal, or hero character, or tree, or vehicle, or movie scene. I can guarantee you, your conversation partner will either agree and run with it or disagree and pick one they like better and then you run with that!

The essence of this is creativity and discovery—also known as fun.

CHAPTER 8

Curiouser and Curiouser

"Sell your cleverness and buy bewilderment."

-Rumi (Persian poet, 1207-1273)

When I worked in a large corporation a while back, it was obvious to me, as it surely would be to any functioning adult, that my boss was a control freak, my job was a mess, and I was a misunderstood artist. This felt true, correct, obvious, no other way to explain it.

As you may have guessed, these were my interpretations. Let's talk about the boss. What she does is send me an email every other day asking me what progress I am making on this one project. This appears to me to be micromanagement. However, these exact same circumstances might be seen, by someone else, as the acts of a supportive boss.

I tell you this in the effort to portray a big, strange truth. There is no single truth. Every one of us has our idiosyncratic individual interpretation of the world. But as soon as we realize this, we forget it. Like right now. Even if I know people have their own ideas, mine are better. Oh yes, I know everyone has their own individual interpretation. But I am right about how much better dark chocolate is then milk chocolate. And what young people should and should not wear. And how we should behave at the airport luggage carousel.

The reason I am bringing this up, in the context of listening, is most of us are in the habit of thinking we already know what the speaker is talking about.

If I say, "My boss is a control freak!"

You might say, "Oh yeah. I know exactly what that's like. My boss is too! She makes us wear locator devices... "

On one hand, perhaps you're coming from a noble idea of wanting to commiserate with me. But you are assuming that you know what I feel like. You may have had very similar feelings, fair enough. However, you have not quite listened yet. You have not yet "gotten" or understood or been curious about my particular experience, as in, "That sounds challenging. Tell me more."

Thinking that you already know about whatever the topic is, can make you dismissive of the other person's experience. Or could make you turn the conversation back to yourself. Oops.

Even if you already know exactly what they felt like and exactly their experience (which is impossible) you will not have listened. The act of letting them speak and you witnessing them is where the magic happens. For that, you get to try on wonderment, inquisitiveness, and curiosity about what's happening for them.

Antidote for Judgment: Curiosity

We talked earlier about how we human beings have this internal voice called "The Judge." It follows that many of the decisions and opinions we have about ourselves, and others are negative.

It's not even personal to us as individuals, this negativity. It's a survival mechanism called "Be suspicious & doubting first. This will keep you safe." Your ability for automatic negative judgment is not in question here. You're probably great at it.

But for a rich fulfilling life, turning down the volume on that fearful voice is a big part of this adventure. One specific way to turn around that negative voice, to reduce that judgmental take, is to practice being curious.

Curiosity is defined as "a strong desire to know or learn something." Synonyms for it are inquisitiveness, interest, spirit of inquiry. Maybe even nosiness. Yes, I am going to put it right out there. Let's try on some nosiness. Not as in snooping for scandal but as in concern about a person's experience, how they interpret things, how they view the world. I would characterize it as caring about your friend's life and their feelings. You are interested in, and want to be helpful to, them.

The second definition of the word curiosity is "a strange or unusual object or fact." As in, "The tour guide showed us some of the curiosities of the haunted house." More synonyms are: Peculiarity, oddity, unusual, rarity, marvel, wonder. A curio.

- What if I am unusual?
- What if you are a curio?
- What if your sibling is a rarity?
- What if your boss is a marvel?

Doesn't that change how you might interact with them?! What an interesting, baffling, unusual creature, in a good way, this is across from me. This approach reminds me that I do not know much about them nor their experience. I can focus on the speaker and be on the lookout for their specialness.

You may have heard of "Curious George"? He's a young monkey, from a series of children's books, written in the 1940s, who lives in the city with his best friend, The Man in the Yellow Hat. George is a brilliant example of the fun and adventures that come from being inquisitive, an explorer, an investigator. I have a picture of him on my desk to remind me to dive in.

Many Shades of Curiosity

The word I like best here is "wonder." Why? Because I cannot possibly know what other people are feeling and thinking—neither can you. Only by listening from a place of curiosity and wonder can we even start to "get it."

For instance, I was recently working with a colleague, Rinda, and she said to me "I really want this project to be a success". My immediate thought was, "Well, DUH! Of course, we want this to succeed." As you can tell, not coming from curiosity. My next thought was,

"Ugh. I bet she wants me to get my part of the project done early and into PowerPoint before she has to ask me for it." What listening is that? Yup, Level 1.

Then I remembered, get curious.

I said, "I wonder, what does success look like to you?"

She said, "Tons of money!"

"Right!" I agreed. "And what else?"

Rinda thought for a moment and then said, "You know when I feel most successful is when a client refers me to a friend of theirs. At the end of this, I'd like Joanne to feel she could recommend us."

Aha! How different than what I thought.

We went on to have a conversation about how we, together, could create the outcome she was dreaming of. Later I did tell her I thought she'd meant for me to get my PowerPoint to her early. She laughed and said, if she expected that she'd be waiting a long time. Hmph.

But a couple of things strike me about that conversation. One, I thought I knew what she meant. I did not. If I hadn't asked, we would have continued working together having different ideas about what a successful project outcome would be. Result: we might have been less successful, and we might not have come through it such good friends.

Second, that conversation about having a client recommend us, was rich and deep and inspiring. That's where the phrase—I WONDER—really helped me to slow myself down and listen.

I have a coaching client, Kevin, who is a terrific manager in a large service industry company. I'm working with him because he is a star, and his company wants to elevate his leadership. A few days ago, he described to me a meeting where he experimented with spreading leadership roles throughout the team, the way he'd wanted to.

I said, "Sounds like a real achievement" doing my best reflecting back.

"No," he said. "I'm failing."

I was so surprised. I was tempted to say, "No you're not!" But that's a Level 1 response—my opinion, trying to tell him he's fine. That is not listening.

"I'm curious Kevin. How are you failing?"

Wild, right? I am trusting what he's saying and I'm curious about his experience, his definitions, his meaning. People are endlessly fascinating and complex. Once you trust that there is depth and experience in each person, that "there is a there, there," listening gets so much easier.

Might you be wondering what Kevin replied? Perfect! That's what curiosity does. Makes you even more curious. But I'm saving his answer for the sequel to this blockbuster book of mine.

"Be curious, not judgmental."

-Walt Whitman (Author of *Leaves of Grass*, 1819-1892)

-Ted Lasso (TV show, *Ted Lasso*, 2020)

Positivity, Shmopsitivity

Early in my training as a coach, one of the workshop instructors announced that really, the point of coaching was to support people in living lives of fulfillment. Fulfillment as in personal values, life purpose, strengths, vision, passion, talents.

I raised my hand and said, "What the hell are you talking about? Aren't people supposed to work all day and all night, at the best paying job they can fake their way into, that has a good retirement plan, and still fret about money? This coaching stuff is so we can help them manage the stress of that. Right?"

Anna Maria said, "Well, not exactly. In fact, what we're saying is a bit radical. Rather than pursue what seems secure or safe, from someone else's point of view, the idea here is to look inside. To reflect on what matters to you individually. What makes you, one-of-a-kind, specifically, personally, fulfilled? What lights you up? What's a good use of you?"

Well, this was a stunner. Never heard this before. You mean, I have an internal world that matters? "Yeah? And pigs can fly." said my Me Channel. But I wanted it to be true. Here's what I discovered.

In many parts of our lives, we look for what's not working. The effort behind this can be noble: to improve, to do better, to make progress. But always looking in the direction of problems has us feel that's all there is. Talk about overwhelming. To wake up every day to mistakes and doubts and idiots is a rough trek.

Anna Maria continued, "Wise people the world over encourage us to look toward what is working. To appreciate, to encourage, to enthuse."

"What about?" I had to ask. "The sun's exploding pretty soon anyway. I took astronomy classes."

"Lauren, that's a perfect example of looking at what's not working. Well done." I felt encouraged. How clever was that? Anna Maria didn't say I was correct in my assessment, but she made me right. She included me even if what I said was a buzzkill.

However, my personal instructions-for-life handbook included deep dark suspicions about "positivity." Optimists are either trying to sell you something or have gone off their medications. I have a *New Yorker* cartoon on my bulletin board that, for me, sums this up. One little mouse is in a tiny wagon which is tied to a string. At the other end of the string, pulling along the wagon and giving the mouse a ride down the hall, is a large cat. Another teeny mouse is calling out from the mouse hole, "Think! Why is she being so nice to you?"

What to Talk About

Come to find out, I'd fallen prey to the prevailing mood of the news cycle. Things are bad and only getting badder, baddest, apocalyptic-est. For over 100 years now, we've been flooded with assessments and psychoanalysis and serial killer shows that focus on neurosis, afflictions, deficits. All problems, all the time focused on the question of "What is wrong here?"

Fortunately, a couple of decades ago, psychologists, environmentalists, social researchers started pushing back. Instead of assuming we're all broken, let's focus on what works about us. When we assume we are whole and strong the question shifts to "What is working here?"

Out of this movement came more focus and support for the personal values, strengths, resilience, and creativity that humans possess. We are pretty remarkable creatures, self-doubt aside. When you are listening to your comrade, the invitation is to tune in to what is admirable, generative, impressive about them.

This is an appreciative approach. What strengths do I notice in my conversation partner? My sister is logical. My husband is generous. My father is disciplined. My boss is a communicator. (All those emails.) I can bring this up to them, reflect back to them in conversation, the strength I know they have.

You can also point to what your friend enjoys doing, what he values. What quality of life does he engage with that you can reflect back to him? Perhaps he likes adventure. Or serenity. Laughter. Achievement. Freedom.

Fortunately, my early concerns about fake positivity or shallow cheerleading were swept away when I learned about this appreciative approach. This method is meant to balanced, authentic, and helpful. You are demonstrating to your friend or colleague that you truly hear, see, and know them.

One of the many challenges about other people, though, is that they are unpredictable. The topics they bring up will vary. Some conversations may move into uncomfortable terrain. I do have certain sensitivities and concerns that can make listening well a challenge. You probably have your own list too. I imagine each of us with a hierarchy of topics that increase the difficulty of Listening Out Loud. By difficulty I mean the ability to hold onto your equanimity, your capacity to remain focused on Level 2 rather than Level 1.

Even so, with the variety and surprises of the conversational experience, listening well looks the same in all of them. For example, a middling challenge might be that your comrade wants to talk (complain) about another person. As an Out Loud Listener you can totally handle this. You get curious about their experience, and you reflect back what you're hearing. You don't have to vote or agree, if you like or don't like, the third party. You simply use your Level 2 Listening as you normally would.

To my mind, the Extreme Sports end of the difficulty scale is when I am on the receiving end of feedback or criticism. Nothing like being given a shellacking to press all the Me Channel buttons. So, what do you do? First, take in some air, a deep in-breath and a slow exhale. This can help through the entire conversation to pace your breathing, to calm your nervous system. Remind yourself this is about their experience, their interpretation and less about you as a failure of a human being. There also could be the tiny hope that you'll learn something useful. Then, as best you can, mirror back to them what they are expressing to you.

Same thing when you find yourself in a conflict or argument. This is the deeper Hero's Journey, certainly. To be a good listener when your own feelings are reeling takes a certain maturity and courage. The more you use these skills, the more prepared you are to meet the most complicated listening challenges with ease and aplomb.

> "This is what I learned: that everybody is talented, original and has something important to say."
>
> -Brenda Ueland (Author of
> *If You Want to Write*, 1891-1985)

Play Date

Back in my more self-centered days, I didn't often think deeply about other people. If they were in front of me, fine. But pondering them, from a distance? Waste of time. Turns out, being "thoughtful" does mean having thoughts about other people. Not just judgmental opinions but wondering daydreams and extrapolations.

What to wonder about? Since you'll be in your own head for this exercise, you can consider all kinds of things about other people. Activating your curiosity muscle is what we're up to here. Here's a question list that I've found helpful. Maybe take your favorite person and have a wonder about them.

- What do they value / find important in life?

- What empowers them?

- What makes them sad?

- What makes them laugh?

- How are they hard on themselves?

CHAPTER 9

Finely Tuned Instrument

"The only way to disarm a human being is by listening."

-Glennon Doyle (American author, 1976–present)

When I was hired to lead coaching workshops, I took that to mean I knew what I was doing. First mistake. Fortunately, the on-boarding process was rigorous. Before teaching, I was to attend each class again as an observer, of the master instructors who were leading it. This won't take too long, I thought, I'll be ready to go, like, tomorrow.

My first day of the Coaching Fundamentals workshop arrives. It's a three-day course, and I've traveled to Northern California for my immersion experience. I'm staying in the hotel where the course is offered so simply skip down the stairs and I'm there. The room has a large window, thankfully, and the 24 chairs are set in a circle awaiting the participants. Lena and Derek, the master co-instructors, greet me with delight and my happy meter is buzzing. I settle myself in the back of the room with Diet Coke and granola bars—breakfast of champions.

The first exercise in the course is a mingle; it's meant to do a couple of things. One is to have people meet each other, let them move around and relax. Another is that it creates the mood for coaching. Because the question posed, for all to answer, is "What is a dream or vision you have for your life?" Not "What do you do?" or "How are you?" but straight into the big stuff.

To start the mingle, participants stand up and find a partner. They ask each other "What is your dream?" and each have a 2-minute conversation answering it. Then switch to a new partner for another 2-minute conversation. Then another switch—this rotation happens up to ten times. What's predictable about this exercise is people start out quiet and timid but by the end are laughing and hooting and sharing their fondest hopes.

Once everyone sits back down, it's time to talk about the exercise; what people experienced and learned. Several folks in a row commented on the surprising speed with which the conversation went deep. How, in just a minute, with a stranger, trust was there. Lots of nods and smiles around the room. In my little back corner, I am basking in the glow.

Just then, another participant, in a loud carrying voice proclaims that, "This is not real trust! Trust cannot be produced that fast."

In my head, I yell, "Yes it can! These people are telling you it can. I've felt it myself. What do you know anyway?"

Fortunately, the real instructor, Lena, knew what to do. "It certainly can take time to build trust."

The participant, who'd been ready to do battle, sat back in his chair and took a deep breath. Everyone in the room took a breath. And on we went to the next exercise.

I was floored. I'd been prepared to tell him exactly what was what—that I was right, and he was not. A Level 1 listening move if ever there was one. Maybe I wasn't quite ready to lead these courses after all.

Lena must know some form of jujitsu, I figured, where the energy of the enemy is used against them somehow. No, she explained later. She simply accepted what Daniel had to say. Importantly she didn't see him as the enemy or in need of correction, but as a fellow human with a valid opinion. Lena found what she could line up with in what he said and made him right.

Accepting (Is Not Agreeing)

The superpower that Lena was flexing was accepting what was said, finding what she could say yes to in it. Not agreeing, as in "Yes, that's right." But in accepting, as in "Yes, I understand your perspective."

Our current fascination with public drubbings, outings, shamings, and cancellings makes me want to be crystal clear. The kind of listening we're pursuing here is one-on-one—between you and one other person. Not on social media, not in public, not about proving a point, not about sowing conflict and outrage.

Listening Out Loud is designed to build connection and understanding. For your close circle of people—the relationships that affect your satisfaction in life. Will the generous shifts you make with them ripple out into the wider world? Absolutely, yes. Changing the world starts with you, yourself, and yours. Not the other way around.

That said, it's still a kick in the head to accept someone else's opinion. Yes, we know intellectually that none of us agree on everything. But holy smoke, so often winning-through-rightness can feel like the only thing that matters. It's as if my opinions get wound around the axle of my survival instinct. You challenge my thinking, I'll come out fighting.

From a Listening Out Loud perspective, acceptance of what your compatriot is expressing means you comprehend it. It does not mean you like, support, or agree with said opinion. But you grasp it. In this way you can defuse tension, reduce defensiveness, and create a safe space, regardless of the multiple and differing opinions that might be swirling about you. Think about the power of that for a moment.

The ability to accept is an extraordinarily mature approach to conversation. Regrettably, I am not any kind of mature. But I have decided to work on it. Because the reality is that in our relationships, particularly marriages, upwards of 70% of our disagreements are not resolvable. This alarming factoid comes from John Gottman a marriage researcher who knows what there is to know about this. He's practically psychic; his Love Lab can predict with 93% accuracy the couples who will divorce. What matters, says the wise John Gottman, is how you and your partner cope with the irresolvable. In other words, how accepting you are of each other.

I will admit to a level of self-satisfaction, an inner pride, when I can accept what a colleague with whom I devoutly disagree is saying to me. Maybe I even feel a bit superior. Because she, and her opinions, are hers. I am still me, over here with my own ideas, and still had her feel heard. I understood her, gave her permission to be where she is, welcomed her real thoughts. I may not like them, but my approval is not the point.

This energy of acceptance is what can create, sometimes, enough space to explore a variety of perspectives. When I don't have to defend my ideas, there's more of a chance they might shift. But that's not the reason to do it. Remember the 70% Not-To-Be-Resolved? The point of acceptance is that the relationship remains solid.

Volume Knobs

A big part of Emotional Intelligence is being aware of your internal landscape. Really noticing what you are thinking and what you are feeling. From this awareness you can choose your focus. Whether to continue with attention on yourself or to extend your listening to include someone else.

We usually have Level 1 at top volume and don't notice that is what's happening. That inner monologue just runs on automatic unless we use the rest of our brain to intervene. Now that you know there is a Level 2 Listening, you have the choice to manage your own attention.

I like to think of these two types of listening as volume knobs. On old-fashioned TVs and radios there was a round physical knob that you could turn to the left to lower volume and turn to the right to amplify sound. You could also turn knobs for more or less treble and more or less bass. You had control of the quality of sound. Just as you can control the quality of your listening.

When I was a little kid, my dad purchased a fancy stereo system that was all one piece of furniture. Of course, it was very special and not to be touched. My older brother told me a secret about it though. That the volume wasn't working right. If you wanted the sound to be quiet, you had to turn the knob to its top position. And if you wanted to blast it, you had to put the knob all the way in the other direction. You see where this is going?

One day my mom had a couple of nice ladies over for lunch. My 5-year-old self thought it would be lovely to have a little music. So, I asked if I could turn on the radio for them. My mom said, yes. The ladies smiled at me.

I skipped over to the stereo, turned the volume knob all the way to the top, and turned it on. Out of the speakers Paul McCartney screamed "Get back! Get back to where you once belonged!" As I turned to run, hands over my ears, I saw my mother throw herself on the stereo. I tore straight through the house, out the back door, and hid under the porch.

So, this whole idea about knobs really has some deep significance for me. My point is that we can let our Level 1 Listening take up all the space in our head. It becomes all we can hear, like The Beatles for me, and the nice ladies, that day.

Once I got more complete information about how the volume knob actually worked, I had more control over the whole thing. That's what I want for you—to be able to dial down the Level 1 Listening when you want to and to dial up your Level 2 Listening when you want to.

I don't mean that Level 1 is wrong. There are profoundly important processes that Level 1 makes possible. It's how we understand the language we speak, it's how we interpret what's going on around us, it's how we remember our experiences and lives. Especially when it's our turn to talk about ourselves, Level 1 is right there with us.

Certainly, the human brain is amazing. But it also likes shortcuts and taking naps. It can get a little sloppy and let the Judge take over. It could use some exercise to stay in shape. Listening well, at Level 2, expands the capabilities of our brains. We think new thoughts, learn surprising things, create new synapses and Aha-moments for ourselves and the people we are listening to.

Am I telling you that if you turn up your Level 2 Listening that you will get smarter? Yes. Yes, I am. And you'll be a lot smarter than I was about the radio.

"A good listener is not only popular everywhere, but after a while he knows something."

-Wilson Mizner (Playwright, 1876-1933)

Interrupting Well

My sister and I recently realized that we belong to a family of mono-logists. If that were a positive, it might mean we're good storytellers or that we're entertaining. What we mean, is when one of us gets going, we have a lot to say with no real need to include anyone else. My dad's forte is the harangue, my brother's is reenactment, my sister is death by 1000 details. Mine is random stream-of-consciousness connections. A book is probably a monologue too?

So let me say, you do NOT have to sit silently waiting for your conversation partner to run out of air before you can say anything. That's too hard on both of you. Yes, you heard me right. The both of you. It's hard on the speaker, too, because the validation that comes from being paid attention to, often results in them going and going and going. Even if they know they are off-point or repeating them-selves or just plain boring. They have you captive so on they talk. A monologist doesn't know about the importance of being in relation-ship with you, of the learning that comes from going back and forth. You as a listener, just waiting, are not feeling useful or included or even needed really. Next time you see them coming toward you, you'll probably hide.

The rule, though, about not interrupting, only arises when the world believes the only way to respond is from Level 1. Meaning that, in the past, when you interrupted it's likely you'd make the conversation about you. Of course, a colleague is going to try to get in everything they want to say before you ruin it by turning the spotlight back on you. You can see how this becomes more of a competitive sport than a real conversation.

What's different here is that you are not reacting from Level 1, you're coming from Level 2. You're interested in their experience, so you are interrupting to deepen the conversation, not divert it. That means you have a job to do. You're engaging with the speaker in reflecting back what you're hearing, noticing the emotion they're experiencing, and sharing empathetic observations.

Let's use the infamous Prince of Denmark, *Hamlet* as our shining example of someone who could have used an interruption. He rambles on and on for hours. Stay or go? To be or not to be? Kill or be killed? And after all those in-his-head-gymnastics, it really does not end well. Hamlet needed a fantastic, interruptive listener to help him sort through his options and choices.

We, as amazing listeners, cannot just wait around until our friend is done talking to do that. Please, please, please, after they've gotten out maybe five sentences, it is your turn to talk. In order for you to stay engaged, in order for the conversation to deepen, in order for the other person to feel listened to, you need to speak.

Here are some ways to do it:

- "I'd like to pause us for a moment..."
- "Let me see if I'm understanding you..."
- "I want to check in here..."
- "What you just said sounds important..."

I want to underline that you are not a victim here, having to listen to someone until they peter out. You are a co-creator in this conversation. Neither of you has a script you're reading from. You are making this up together as you go. Help them talk it through, help them see things they didn't before. It's not hard—you just have to jump in.

And yes, it can feel a bit like leaping from the high dive, until you get used to it. Which is why it's important to recognize when you approach this from Level 2 it's not really interrupting. It's more like engaging. If you're in a game of ping pong you are not waiting around for the other person to get tired of hitting the ball before you start playing. You are engaged, hitting the ball back, responding to their offers. It's the same with conversation.

Which reminds me of another possible concern. Should I finish people's sentences?

I have in my past, when I was not a good listener, finished people's sentences for them. Because they were speaking too slowly or what they were saying was completely obvious or I was showing how smart I was... You see? When I'm coming from a Level 1 need to prove something, then I'm not being a good listener. Rather, I'm being insulting.

However, now, I hang around a lot of other coaches. They are fabulous listeners. I really recommend them as friends. I love it when they finish my sentences because that means they "get" what I am saying and "get" me.

See how much our internal mindset matters? If I'm finishing sentences because I'm being judgmental that will distance my conversation partner. But if I'm really following another person and listening closely from Level 2, finishing their sentences could have them feel deeply understood. And, if I finish their sentence incorrectly, it's okay. They let me know and on we go!

Time and Place Matters

Timing the conversation well is far more important than most of us give it credit for. Somehow, we think we're supposed to be ready any time for any kind of conversation. No. For anything more complex than "Do you want the dressing on the side?" set a time and place so the two of you can focus, pay attention.

Even if it's a five-minute chat—give yourself the best possible chance to have it be an effective short talk rather than a fast, mistake-filled, misinterpretation episode that leaves both of you irritated.

If a co-worker stops you in the hall or pops their head in your cube and asks you a question you do not have to answer! What you can say is, "I have a deadline just now, could we talk at 3:00?" Or "This sounds important, I want to give it my attention, how about lunch tomorrow?"

Be brave! Manage your time so that you can really listen. This is a quality issue. Likewise, if someone you want to talk to asks to schedule a time, respect that. And expect that you will be paid close attention to then.

Let's talk about place too. Privacy and quiet are ideal when you want to Listen Out Loud. All too often we're on the phone or computer screen, where distractions abound. I must turn off every ping, bell, clonk, and pong so that I can focus. Also, I like to make sure that people like me, eavesdroppers, aren't hanging around.

Check with your conversation partner, too, if they feel comfortable where they are. If you're able to meet in person, decide together on a good place for a conversation. You're designing the surroundings so you both can pay attention well.

Here's a daring idea for you. If an individual calls you on the phone and you are not ready to talk, Do Not Answer It. You are in charge of YOU and your time and what you spend it on. You can be trusted to respond sooner or later, yes? Do it when you're ready, have time, and can focus on them.

I'm realizing that what I'm talking about here is respect. Formally defined respect means "to hold in esteem or honor." Listening closely, giving yourself the time and place to do so, shows that you want to honor the conversation.

Emotional Intelligence on Parade

Your level of self-awareness matters here; your ability to observe what's happening with you as you interact with another person. Not in a self-conscious, self-critical way but toward supporting you as an outstanding listener for your conversation partner. To get a little flowery, the idea is: Self as Instrument of Change.

When you (yes, you, specifically and in particular) are aware of the power you have to matter in other people's lives, through conversations large and small, courage wins. The hero's path of improving your ability to accept, to interrupt, to engage fully in another's perspective, counts as being the change you want to see in the world.

Play Date

This play date is a multiple-choice option. You may already accept other's opinions easily and could use some practice with interrupt/engage. Or the other way around.

From this list of opportunities, you get to pick the hardest, the easiest, the most needed, the least needed, or whatever other criteria you like.

Practice small experiments. Some will work great, others might not. It's all good because you are moving toward spectacular listening. Every experience teaches.

- Accept vs. Agree

- Interrupt/Engage

- Turn Down Level 1 / Turn Up Level 2

- Choose Quality Time and Place

CHAPTER 10

Must I Care?

"Listening, not imitation, may be
the sincerest form of flattery."

-Dr. Joyce Brothers (Psychologist
and writer, 1927-2013)

I'd never have made it as a listener, if I had to be enlightened in any way. I'd have flunked, bombed out completely. Luckily with listening, though, you get to start wherever you are. Maybe you floss, maybe not. Maybe you do yoga, maybe you don't. Maybe your chakras are shiny clean, or not so much. Doesn't matter. No renovations of you are required.

One of my mottos in life is: Keep the Bar Low. I just want to step over the hurdle rather than make a sweaty running leap at it. No high jumps. For me, to make listening special or difficult or unapproachable defeats the purpose of its existence. As you already know by now, I'd like more people in good conversations, enjoying themselves, starting right now.

So, if words like empathy and compassion feel too hard, forget them. If you like them and they encourage you, keep them close. But you do not have to be any virtuous thing before you start with Listening Out Loud.

That'd be like saying you should only exercise if you are already fit. No, at any weight or size or ability, we can move, and play, and dance. And receive the benefits of exercise in return. Same with listening. Everyone can Listen Out Loud. Start where you are and let the benefits roll in.

One of the advantages of this kind of listening? You might develop some empathy. No pressure. But I want to warn you; it could happen. Once I had some words to use, to do effective listening, that at least gave the impression that I cared, I liked it.

As I practiced, I felt comfortable, more often, that I'd be okay in conversations. My Level 1 worry about "what will we talk about" stopped taking up so much room. This relaxed me and gave me more space to appreciate how much we humans have in common.

Being Heard

In the 1960's some genius types at MIT were playing with the idea of robots and artificial intelligence (AI). This was early in the history of computers, but they were curious if humans could ever think that an AI was actually human. (Have you seen the 1982 film, *Bladerunner*? That scene with Rutger Hauer putting a nail through his hand. And the "Tears in Rain" speech? I love androids.)

A professor at MIT, Joseph Weizenbaum, invented the first chatbot. He and his graduate students chose a simple conversational structure for the bot to follow. The program only ended up including 100 lines of code. Want to guess what the chat template was? Carl Rogers' Active Listening technique.

The chatbot, named ELIZA, is in a computer on a desk near Weizenbaum's MIT offices. Say I want to have a therapeutic chat with her. I pull up a chair and type in "I'm feeling sad." Of course, the program is designed to pick up on keywords of emotion like "sad." ELIZA would respond in writing, "I'm sorry you're feeling sad. Tell me more." It can simply use my word and offer it back in a statement or question. Along with a few other standard questions to use in a pinch, ELIZA and I are rolling.

Here's a look at an actual transcript of one of ELIZA's conversations.

Julie: "Men are all alike"

ELIZA: "In what way?"

Julie: "They're always bugging us about something or other."

ELIZA: "Can you think of a specific example?"

Julie: "Well, my boyfriend made me come here."

ELIZA: "Your boyfriend made you come here?"

Julie: "He says I'm depressed much of the time... I do need help!"

Turns out that Weizenbaum's secretary, I've named her Julie, was a huge fan of ELIZA. She regularly interacted with ELIZA and at one point, asked the professor to leave his own office so that she might have a private chat. And it wasn't just Julie. Turns out people lined up around the block to engage with ELIZA. Even the students who helped develop the program, who knew exactly how the chatbot was designed, wanted their chance to talk with ELIZA.

What are the implications of this? My take is that the folks engaging with ELIZA felt safe, that they wouldn't be judged. They were taken seriously, their ideas considered, their worries legitimated. They were being drawn out, out of the gerbil wheel of the mind. Invited to speak, to explore, to learn as they went.

There are simply too few places in life where we are really listened to. It's such a glorious, helpful relief to express myself and to be "gotten" by someone, something outside of me. Most of my life I've kept journals, writing out my messes. That's one level of expression. In my teenage years, our St Bernard dog, Fred, was my warm-hearted friend. As I spoke to him, he'd tilt his large head and gaze at me with his sad eyes. Whether I was laughing or crying, he'd lick my face. Very helpful to me. If I'd been given the chance to type my feelings into a soul-less computer and have it facilitate a conversation to look more deeply into my experience, I'd be a yes to that.

However, this is not at all what Weizenbaum foresaw. He thought that this experiment would be funny. That the conversation would be so simplistic and shallow, that no one would be interested. And worries about robots taking over the world would be moot. Weizenbaum was appalled by ELIZA's popularity. He worried that people were being taken in by the program, believing there was a there. For him, when the machine says, "I understand"—that's a lie. There is no "I" at the other end of the conversation.

But I think he missed the point. People want to be listened to. In whatever way they can get it. If few people in our lives will listen, typing into a machine that helps air out feelings and uncover a few insights is a good option. Sherry Turkle, a colleague of Weizenbaum's at MIT, interpreted why people loved ELIZA this way: "At the time, I thought they were using it as an interactive diary... to get their feelings out."

What listening can mean for people is a chance to express their feelings, an opportunity to move them out of the body and mind. Which can lessen the power of negative feelings and increase the power of the positive. Even taking the time to type into an impersonal computer their deepest experiences and concerns shows how useful the exercise is. Once the thoughts and feelings are in the ethers, there's alchemy afoot, a chance for learning, re-orienting, transforming, releasing.

Defining Empathy

Empathy is the capacity to recognize another person's emotions and share in them. When you are listening deeply to another person, you do not need to have gone through the same situation they did. Because empathy is not about connecting to an experience. It is connecting to the emotions that underpin the experience.

Given your own eventful life, using your own knowledge and your imagination, you can guess at what feelings might be happening for someone else. You are absolutely qualified to empathize, to feel for and with another person, because you too have experienced many feelings. From sadness, anger, and embarrassment to pride, enthusiasm, and contentment. So many highs and lows to be had.

You, of course, have your own lens through which you see the world. The specifics of your life shape how you perceive things: Your age, your knowledge, your race, your work, and more, shape how you interpret the world—your Me Channel.

When you are empathizing with another, you are overtly attempting to consider the world from their perspective. Given their background, their challenges, their experiences, how might they feel? Their Me Channel. Here, you are feeling with people. Each of us is completely unique in our experience of the world. Often the best I can do, to connect with you, is imagine what it's like over there with you—to expand my understanding a bit further than just myself.

One last thing. You know how much I care about your mindset. Sometimes the idea of empathy gets mixed up with sympathy. Brene Brown, who's written innumerable terrific books, has a good description of the difference between the two. Simply put, sympathy tends to include feeling sorry for someone else. Oddly, this can create a separation. If I feel that my friend is different than I am and I'm uneasy that something bad happened to them, I feel pity and guilt. That is not what they are feeling. It's what I am feeling. From this point of view, I might try to cheer them up or tell them it's for the best or whatever other platitude comes to mind. But that's a Level 1 trick focused on making me feel better, not them.

Empathy, however, is more of a vicarious experience, an identification with the emotions of another. If you and I are talking, as an Out Loud Listener, I'll try to align myself with your feelings, to understand your experience. If you softly say, "I took my little dog into the vet last week just for a regular checkup. I still can't believe this, but the doctor says she has cancer." Rather than saying, "I'm sure it'll be fine" I'd respond, "Oh no. What a terrible surprise. Such a happy pup shouldn't be so sick."

My mindset, in order to listen well, is that we are in this together and together we are strong enough to look at what is happening. Empathy is relating to the emotion my friend is articulating. Then sharing my understanding of that feeling.

One key to deeper relationships is the ability to stay with feelings. Not try to change or deny what is being felt. Coming from a stiff upper lip tradition myself, I'm still working on this. But really, whether the emotions are light or dark, we don't have to assume they're a problem, that something is wrong that needs to be fixed. When we engage with them together, we can be allies, adventurers, collaborators in the highs and lows of life.

> "Listening fast and caring immediately
> is a skill in itself."
>
> -Amanda Palmer (Performance Artist, 1976–present)

Steps Toward Empathy

There's a classic saying: "Be kind. Everyone you meet is carrying a heavy burden." I've seen it attributed to Plato, to Socrates, to Philo of Alexandria. But actually, it's from a 19th century Scottish minister who wrote popular inspirational books under the name, Ian McLaren.

At first, I was disappointed by this. You know, I wanted the heft of an ancient Greek philosopher behind me here. But perhaps only a more modern, generous person could offer us such an inclusive idea. (The Greeks owned slaves and stabbed their politicians in public—just saying.)

Cultivating kindness is one of the first ways to develop empathy. What I want to add on to this wisdom is that it's important to start with yourself. Be kind to yourself. You are also carrying a burden. You are included in who to be kind to.

You might have internal trash talk habits that are harsh & judgmental, like, "You are a waste of space." Most of us shame, belittle, and criticize ourselves in ways we'd never think of doing to others. It's not fair, nor acceptable.

My sense is that the internal inner critic, that Judge voice is a voice for disconnection and separation. The more you let it run you, the less you get to enjoy life. Better to be warm and understanding toward ourselves when we suffer, fail, or feel inadequate. We get to practice kindness on ourselves so that we can offer it to others as well.

Another way to develop empathy is to admit that each individual human deserves a measure of dignity and respect. You do not have to like the people you speak with. You can have important, deeply felt conversations with just about anyone. Particularly when you have made a conscious decision that the person who is speaking is deserving, is worth a bit of your time and attention.

One way to help with that is to find a positive about your relationship or something positive about that person. Again, you don't have to befriend them but finding something to admire can reorient your feelings toward them.

I have this one colleague who makes me nervous. She's on the lookout for mistakes, really gets into the details, and I know I will be found wanting. One of my least favorite experiences. So, do I go out for beers with her? No. But I can appreciate that she strives for excellence. She has the patience for every detail. She takes care of things that I detest. Finding the positive about her, helps me stay in conversation with her, allows me to "feel" for her, rather than focusing on my own judgments about her.

Lastly, in your efforts to become more empathic (or empathetic, both words mean the same thing) you can consciously create the intention in yourself that you will listen well. Too often we stumble into a conversation with no game plan, no objective, except, "How do I get out of this?"

Many books on the topic of conversation, whether addressing Difficult or Crucial or Fierce or Uncomfortable conversations, all agree: have a conscious intention for how you want a conversation to go. An important step in being successful is to really consider, "What do I want to have happen?"

In BJ Fogg's book *Tiny Habits*, he describes a woman, Amy, who'd recently divorced. It was ugly, acrimonious. Every hand off of the children was a fight. Meanwhile, Amy, was trying to grow her own business and the negative exchanges wrecked her productivity. She'd re-fight, re-insult, re-spin for the rest of the day, even lose sleep at night.

What she wanted, instead, was to retain her focus and energy, not be thrown off balance. Amy decided on a small experiment. Whenever she felt insulted by her ex-, she wouldn't respond. She would, instead, chose a nice thing to do for herself. A cup of tea at her favorite place, play an uplifting song, watch a new movie. Instead of reacting, she'd say to herself, "Oh look, another insult. Guess it's time for a manicure."

This allowed her to stay calm and focus on her own business. No replaying of the conversation or emotional upset to be dealt with. In a strange way, her ex was prompting her to take care of herself. Insults as self-care gifts. Eventually, as Amy no longer played along, he lost interest in fighting and gave up on the insults.

My favorite part of the story is that, after this experience, Amy developed compassion for her former husband. She realized that she'd been a social buffer for him in their marriage and now he was having to learn, on his own, how to engage productively. Amy sensed how challenging, even alarming this was for him. Her changing attitude allowed them to create a more equable dynamic, particularly for their children. Amy set her intention for how these interactions would flow and created a long-lasting peace.

> "Empathy is the most radical of human emotions."
>
> -Gloria Steinem (American journalist
> & activist, 1934–present)

Being With Others

Years ago, when I was deciding where to get trained as a coach, the reason that I chose the Co-Active Training Institute was this: they offered a workshop for how to be with another person's emotions without having to fix anything. Priceless. One, I can handle people who are having an emotion. Two, I'll know what to do/say in response that will be supportive. Sign. Me. Up.

That is where I learned about the extraordinarily wide variety of emotional experience every one of us has. And this very range of feelings is what makes life rich, meaningful, and worth living. In the past couple of decades research into emotions and emotional intelligence has flourished. We have more information than ever on how we can experience feelings in positive useful ways and support others in having deeply emotional lives.

Thus, an important part of Level 2 Listening is hearing and naming the emotion that the other person is feeling as they're speaking. The Starter Emotions we've already mentioned are: Sad, Mad, Bad, Glad, & Anxious. As you know, there are far more emotions to be had. Yet we rarely study directly the range of emotions that it's possible to feel.

My experience with emotions, prior to my Co-Active training was that they were happening to me, from out of nowhere, and I wished they'd leave me alone. Putting them away was the job, not looking at them or wondering what they were telling me. Repression as a lifestyle choice.

I didn't know much about the gradations of emotion, until I became a coach. What I learned is that there's a whole range of feelings, from darkest dark to lightest of light, that make life feel textured and full of meaning. The more that each of us can be in-the-moment with our feelings, whether positive or negative, the greater our emotional intelligence, the more self-awareness, the more empathy we have.

We don't have to try and fit our lives inside a narrow window of poker-faced appropriateness. Far too much nonsense is offered up as wisdom in sayings like:

- "If I don't get too excited, I won't get disappointed."
- "Don't be enthusiastic or people will think you're dumb."
- "At work, no one wants to hear you laugh."
- "Smile! It's not that bad."

I'm not suggesting we should go out and pour our emotions all over everybody else. But we humans ought to be able to support other humans in having emotional lives. Including each of us getting better at identifying and experiencing our own emotions. Avoidance is so last century.

It does take a bit of courage to use your empathy skills. You may not be used to it and the people around you may not be used to it. One way to give it a try is by saying, "I want to check in. Sounds like you're feeling ____?" Most people respond with eagerness and more conversation. Expanding your emotional vocabulary is a sure-fire hero move. You'll become more self-aware, and you'll help others be more self-aware. Your nuanced listening will enrich your conversations for good.

There are lovely lists of emotions available these days. I'm including one here that I put together from words that I particularly like. Did I already confess to you that I was an English major? I was basically in a book club for college? Emotions get some terrific words. How about "serene" which means sort of elegantly peaceful. It's on the list. "Bewildered" which I think of as confused and a little hurt, like a puppy you won't play with. Or "exultant" for someone who's achieved a great victory and is proud and joyful. That will be you when you Listen Out Loud.

Play Date

From this lovely list of emotions choose two that you feel frequently and another two you'd like to feel more often. With the people close to you, what emotions do they seem to inhabit and what might they want more or less of, feelings-wise? This is an exercise to do gently; just prompting awareness and range.

Glad	Loving	Playful
Cheerful	Affectionate	Alive
Confident	Friendly	Giddy
Delighted	Kind	Adventurous
Ecstatic	Compassionate	Goofy
Exhilarated	Grateful	Energetic
Glorious	Touched	Jubilant
Elated	Passionate	Invigorated
Joyful	Radiant	Amused
Excited	Tender	Silly
Happy	Moved	Thrilled
Encouraged	Open	Mischievous
Hopeful	Warm	Electrified
Proud	Appreciative	Lively
Exultant	Thankful	Effervescent

Interested	Peaceful	Confused
Astonished	Calm	Torn
Curious	Content	Uncomfortable
Focused	Blissful	Hesitant
Intense	Carefree	Troubled
Absorbed	Centered	Disturbed
Inspired	Expansive	Suspicious
Alert	Free	Restless
Surprised	Grounded	Perplexed
Enthusiastic	Mellow	Uneasy
Inquisitive	Refreshed	Embarrassed
Engrossed	Serene	Unsteady
Intrigued	Satisfied	Skeptical
Fascinated	Relieved	Overwhelmed
Eager	Relaxed	Bewildered

Tired	Scared	Sad	Mad
Fatigued	Afraid	Lonely	Frustrated
Indifferent	Nervous	Disappointed	Aggravated
Lethargic	Insecure	Heavy	Disgusted
Hopeless	Worried	Sorrowful	Resentful
Exhausted	Fearful	Unhappy	Angry
Withdrawn	Helpless	Despondent	Grouchy
Apathetic	Vulnerable	Disheartened	Irritable
Disinterested	Powerless	Blue	Hostile
Bored	Terrified	Dejected	Furious
Reluctant	Alarmed	Grief	Bitter
Detached	Dread	Distressed	Annoyed
Pessimistic	Wary	Brokenhearted	Mean
Sleepy	Frightened	Forlorn	Enraged
Weary	Anxious	Discouraged	Impatient

CHAPTER 11

Discover Together

"Phoeby's hungry listening helped Janie to tell her story."

-Zora Neale Hurston (American author of *Their Eyes Were Watching God* , 1891-1960)

One of my dearest friends, Carrie, is a beacon of living from gratitude and joy. This also means she's a crier. No meetups are complete without a few tears shed about how lucky we are, how much she loves her family and friends, and what a goof she is for dripping from the eyes so often. From her I've learned about appreciation; that life casts delights upon us and when we catch sight of them, some of us leak.

We've always lived in different cities, states even, but met on a work project and have been friends a good long time. In 2015, Carrie had been married to her partner, Kyle, for several years. One of the challenges they faced was grappling with Kyle's Obsessive Compulsive Disorder. His fears were extreme: his loved ones dying, feeling responsible for catastrophes, Carrie having affairs. He didn't talk much about these publicly. But we did have genuinely disgusting chats, over dinner usually, about the diseases you can catch, and how, in public bathrooms. I can't really eat chocolate pudding anymore.

The terrible irony is that Kyle had an affair. After years of worrying and browbeating Carrie, he was the one who fulfilled the fear. Carrie wanted to stay married, to work through this, to mend their troubles.

Kyle wavered, which gave her hope, but he ultimately left. Carrie was devastated; now her tears were all despair.

I finally got to see Carrie in person, several months later; she came to visit us in San Diego for a few days. Naturally, I wanted to hear everything.

"Did I tell you that Kyle told some our friends he was cheating? "

"What, he what?" I sputtered.

"Yeah, he told one of our favorite couples, Carolina and Joey. They knew 6 months before I did. You met them one time. "

"I remember them. They were fun. Real wine lovers, right?"

"That's them. Kyle told them he was having an affair. And made them promise not to tell me."

"Wuh? How? I can't even…"

"Kyle also told my friend Kate. I guess she was friends to both of us. But she was my friend first."

"He is spreading the news around to your friends?! And not telling you?" I asked.

"Yes. He asked Kate not to say anything to me either."

"That's outrageous Carrie."

"I know. Kate decided she wouldn't talk to either of us until Kyle told me. I wondered why she wouldn't get back to me. I'd ask for a time to have a call and she'd never commit. Now I know why,"

"I can't get over what a traitor Kyle turned out to be!" I said.

"I can't get over that my friends didn't tell me."

"Say again?"

"I am so mad that they didn't say anything. They knew for months. And they didn't have the guts to 'fess up."

"Carrie, are you serious?"

"Yes! If I can't count on my friends, who can I count on?" she replied.

"How can you blame them? They were in a terrible position. Kyle tells them something they didn't want to know and then makes them promise to keep it a secret?"

Carrie, put her hand up as if to stop me, and said, "Don't… don't…"

I spoke over her saying, "They are damned if they do, damned if they don't!"

Silently, Carrie left the room and walked out of the house.

I sat there stunned. We'd never been here before; my happy friend so upset she must leave. Of course, I hadn't been listening to her—I had not understood her. My Level 1 interpretation of the situation, and of Kyle, was forefront in my mind. I'd felt so justified in what I was saying. But even if my analysis, my opinion, had merit, that was not listening. What she needed was for me to recognize her experience and be with her first.

About a half hour later, there was a knock at the front door. I opened it, saw Carrie, and we both yelled, "I'm sorry!" at the same time. This set us off together laughing & crying and agreeing to a do-over. Which went much better.

Deepen Learning

That experience was only a few years ago when I was, allegedly, a good listener. What a reminder. The people I feel closest to, I too often treat with less thought and care. Naturally, it's nice to feel secure and easy with my favorite people. But I was careless there, overly committed to my Me Channel, saying whatever I wanted to.

Listening Out Loud means absorbing my compatriot's point of view so I can express it for them, with them. This is what leads to deep understanding. That word "understanding" doesn't seem all that amazing to me. Here's some news though. Harry Reis, a Professor of Psychology at the University of Rochester, specializes in researching social interaction and close relationships. He has found that the one thing that must be present, for a relationship to thrive, is to feel understood.

Trust, love, caring won't carry the day if understanding is missing. To be understood is to be accepted, to belong, to be known. You are mastering that art. When you reflect back what your colleague is expressing, you are engaging in the act of understanding.

However, I want to give you some more tools. Superb listeners, like you, encourage people to continue talking. Not in a breathless monologue but in a conversation of collaborative discovery. You uncover new thoughts, connect dots, ponder, chew over, muse together.

Powerful Questions are that tool. They are Boffo Magic. Your friends, family, and colleagues have rarely been asked questions like these. What's even better is they are not complicated or complex. Powerful Questions are open-ended and usually short—seven words or less. You might even call them dumb, but I prefer Simple, Profound, Elegant. They are not to show what you know but to uncover what your friend knows.

A Powerful Question is not a "yes" or "no" question nor a close-ended one. What I mean by that is a question that somebody can answer with a single word. For instance, "Do you want chips with that?" is not powerful. That's going for a yay or a nay. You can see that it does not encourage more conversation, it doesn't deepen thinking or learning.

There are also ways we put our opinions inside a question format, a Level 1 trick. If your colleague is complaining about her job, you might ask, "You think your job is worse than mine? Or "When are you going to stop kissing up to the boss?" Or "Do you really think you're cut out for this work?" Not Powerful Questions.

Anyway, it's more interesting and enlivening to talk about what is wanted rather than what is not. Indeed, the Law of Attraction suggests that what you pay attention to is what grows. If we focus on only the negative it's likely, we'll get more of that. Not to say that you have to be only positive in your conversation but striking a balance can be helpful.

When you are Listening Out Loud, from Level 2, you could ask:

- What would you really like in your work?
- What would your ideal be?
- What is your dream outcome?
- What does that look like?

My favorite powerful question is "What is important about this?" That question offers a number of useful elements. It suggests to the person you're speaking with that what they are talking about is worthy and you are asking them to report to you why that is so for them. As well, that you want to know them more deeply, you want to hear the answer as to why something matters to them.

The other fantastic thing about this question is all you have to do is change the word "important" and you have any number of powerful questions to ask. So instead of "What is important about this?" you might ask:

- What is [frustrating] about this?
- What is [exciting] about this?
- What is [hard] about this?
- What is [fun] about this?"

Another great all-around question is "What else?" Not, "Is there anything else?" I know it's subtle but that's a yes / no question that implies they should be finished talking. "What else?" assumes there is more to uncover. Also, "Tell me more," while not technically a question, is a terrific encourager in conversation.

Here are my Top Five:

- What do you want? Your ideal?
- What does that look like?
- What is important about this?
- What are you learning?
- What else is here?

In my first year as a coach, I had a big Post-It note hanging on the wall over my desk with these five questions written in huge letters. I could read it from anywhere in the room. On my calls, I'd know that I should ask a question, but I couldn't think of one. So, I would cheat. Look at my Post-It and just read one off.

"Uh... what else?"

And it worked every single time. My recommendation is that you cheat, too. You do not have to remember how to do all of this without any help. You want to have better conversations. That is a noble goal. Use anything and everything that will help you do that. You can look at your notes! No memorization needed.

You can even say things like "Uh oh. That was a yes / no question.

I'd like to take it back. I'm just going to check my Post-It…" Or you can ask your conversation partner, "What should I ask you about?" and let them decide.

This Out Loud Listening thing just gets easier and easier. I just wish I'd remembered that when I was in conversation with my friend Carrie. What could we have found, together, if I'd had my Post-It note?

"The universe buries strange jewels deep within us all and then stands back to see if we can find them."

-Elizabeth Gilbert (American author of *Eat Pray Love*, 1969–present)

GROW for Powerful Questions

In *Coaching for Performance* John Whitmore offers a framework for conversation that I grabbed, stuffed into my backpack, and ran away with. It is treasure map.

GROW is an acronym for a conversation where you are trying to grow the other person. That's the corny part. The terrific part is that it actually works. It is a model you can use for productive interesting conversations, anywhere, anytime, with anyone. Here's what the acronym stands for:

G—Goal

R—Reality (the current situation)

O—Options

W—Way Forward

Each stage offers a chronology of four kinds of powerful questions to ask. The word chronology makes this sound complicated, which I'm sorry about. All I mean is first ask this, second ask that. You'll see.

What we action-oriented humans usually start (and end) a conversation with is DOING. There's a great scene in *The Untouchables* where Sean Connery bellows at Kevin Costner in a strangled Irish (but Scottish) accent, "What are you prepared to DO?" The scene is magnificent.

However, if you haven't watched the rest of the movie, you don't know what Kevin's desired outcome is, what he's working on, what challenges he's facing. Which all matter greatly when deciding what to do, what action to take.

In typical conversations we focus on getting going, on action. That misses quite a bit of significant territory. What are we even solving with this action? Better conversations start with a broader scope. Even if you only have five minutes, opening up the aperture, checking in on the larger context is vital.

For that we have the "G" in GROW which, as you now know, stands for Goal. And the "R" which stands for Current Reality. In short, where are you now (R) and where you want to be (G). These are the places to visit before moving to action. Taking a good look at what is wanted, what is needed, and what the gap is between the vision and the current situation.

For G/Goal here are some questions to use:

- What's your ideal?
- What's your desired outcome?
- Where are you headed?
- What do you want?
- What's the vision?

Often, as you discuss goals, people naturally bring in their present situation. Questions for current R/Reality:

- Where are you now?
- What is helping you move toward what you want?
- What are the obstacles?
- What will it take to make progress?

Elliott Ness, the character Costner plays in *The Untouchables*, works for the U.S. Federal Bureau of Prohibition during the 1920s. He has a major goal and a challenging current reality. Let's pick up with him at the mid-point of the movie and ask him about it:

Us: What's the outcome you're going for, Ness? (Goal)

Ness: Al Capone. He's running Chicago into the ground with his boot-leg liquor trafficking. He's got to be reined in.

Us: Wow, what a challenge to take on. What will that give you, that outcome?

Ness: People can't trust the police or politicians right now. Al Capone has bought all of them. Everything he does is illegal, but he can do what he wants, kill who he wants.

Us: Sounds like you want to clear out the corruption so people can trust again.

Ness: You could say it that way. There's such a thing as the rule of law. We agree to abide by the guidelines we set for ourselves.

Us: What is your current situation? (Reality)

Ness: Well, let's see. I can't trust the Chicago Chief of Police. No one on the police force. Not the mayor.

Us: Those would certainly count as obstacles to your progress. What might be helping you toward your goal?

Ness: I have been able to locate three people, who have joined me in this cause, who cannot be bribed. They have signed on with me.

Us: You sound proud of them.

Ness: Yes and no.

Us: Tell me more.

Ness: One is an accountant.

Us: Oh. That is outside the box.

Ness: But I have faith in the incorruptibility of my team. We are outside of Capone's gangland rule. We'll find a way to bring it down.

Us: I hear you saying that the integrity of your people is an indispensable element in reaching your goal. That how you do this will be as important as what you do.

Ness: True. They're calling us The Untouchables. Capone can threaten us, try to bribe us... but we won't bend.

Us: What will it take to make progress? (Shifting from current Reality to Goal)

Ness: We've got to get creative. The efforts we've made inside the system haven't worked. Something they won't see coming...

We are helping Elliott Ness think through his approach to stopping Al Capone! Yet all we're doing is asking questions. Big wide-open questions. Then reflecting back once in a while. And it's going incredibly well. Uncovering the Goal and the Reality, and diving into them, ideally are 80% of a conversation. We could spend a good deal more time with Ness deepening this conversation, but he's a busy guy.

Moving on to the next part of GROW we arrive at "O" which stands for Options. Options are about actions that could be taken, next steps, people to get help from, resources. As an Out Loud Listener you get to both ask questions and brainstorm ideas in the Options section. You, in no way, have to come up with the right or winning idea. Your role is to play with creativity, wild options, sideways thoughts, to loosen up the approach to a solution. Ask a question, see what your friend says, then you offer an action idea too.

- What could you do?
- What would be easy to do?
- What would be daring?
- What would be fun?
- What could you stop doing?
- Who could help?

Once you've both created some possibilities for action steps, only then is it time for the "What are you going to do?" question. Notice how much there is to discuss before this doing step. Why is that? People follow through, far more often, on the answers they come to themselves. This template, talking through GROW, allows them to see, with more clarity, the playing field they are on and what could work as a next move.

Finally, we've arrived at the "W" in GROW which stands for, you've got it, the Way Forward. This is when commitment happens. Now that we've thoroughly looked at the situation, created some possible action steps, it's time to define the action to take.

- o What's next?
- o What will you do?
- o What will you not do?
- o What is your accountability?

This framework has always been helpful to me. I have a place to come from in asking powerful questions. I know what I'm asking about—either the goal, the current reality, or next steps.

Remember how a hero meets mentors, helpers, supporters on her journey? Well, you're not only a hero for taking on new, challenging skills, you're also a magnificent ally. You can now support other heroes on their way; you're a partner to your colleague's development.

You know, Elliott Ness and his team, given their goal and the limits of their situation developed an unusual approach to catch Capone. Which I'm pretty sure Ness figured out because of his chat with us. While they had tried battling Capone with surprise attacks and violence those only served to escalate the conflict. Instead, the accountant on Ness's team tracked down Capone's accountant, the man who oversaw all the income and outgo. Here the Untouchables found documented proof of old Al's goings-on. How did this, of all things, bring an end to the notorious gangster? He was convicted of tax evasion.

Play Date

Love this exercise! All you need do, in a conversation, is ask Powerful Questions. No reflecting back, just questions.

- What do you want?

- What's your situation now?

- What's the gap you see?

Please note how little you really need to know or say. Your in-the-moment curiosity wins the day.

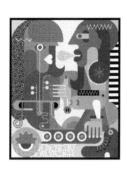

CHAPTER 12

LOL

"May you live every day of your life."
-Jonathan Swift (Irish Author, 1667-1745)

The inspiration for the title of this book, *How To Listen Out Loud*, is two-fold. One is that effective listening means talking, aloud. You probably grasped that by now. The second, though, is a quote from Emile Zola. His name is cool enough on its own, much less that he was a social justice rock star.

I only know about him because I received a greeting card with a quote of his on it. Can I call that serendipity? Or are there gaping holes in my liberal arts education? Did I know of him at one time, but my memory has been diluted by too many carbohydrates?

Anyway, the quote is " I came to live out loud." This card has a permanent spot on my inspirational bulletin board. It speaks to me of courage, joy, vibrancy. Turns out, his writings and his life live up to that quote.

Born in 1840, Zola grew up in poverty and struggled with his schooling. But he went on to become one of France's greatest novelists. From his own experience, he came to believe that every person deserves fair treatment. He did not simply accept the word of those in power, as others of his time did. Zola listened to and believed in the poor and downtrodden. His was an egalitarian and clear-eyed point of view about people and the importance of relationships vs the seductions of power and greed. I may be reaching here but don't you think he must have been a skilled listener?

The highlight of his courage was in January 1898 when he wrote an open letter to the president of France, published on the front page of "L'Aurore" newspaper. Zola was responding to a scandal that had divided France, the Dreyfus Affair. A Jewish French Army officer, Alfred Dreyfus, had been imprisoned for treason. But he was innocent and the victim of a wide-ranging cover-up.

The headline of Zola's article was "J'Accuse...!" ("I accuse"). He pointed the finger at the highest levels of military and government officials, by name, and called them out for their corruption, anti-Semitism, and dishonor. He, in turn, was sued for libel and, fearing he'd also be jailed or worse, he fled France and stayed away for over a year. Ultimately, when he died in 1902, in a suspicious accident, he was considered the conscience of the nation.

What inspires me about Zola's story is his creativity, commitment, and courage. He lived his version of an Out Loud life. His version of a hero's journey. My wish for you, and for me, is that we do that too. To pursue a life full of feeling, relatedness, and meaning; to live your version of OUT LOUD. My promise to you is that Listening Out Loud, will support you in that endeavor.

Little Old Lady?

Nowadays we write to each other constantly. Tweets, emails, texts, IMs. But text-speak can be tricky. Adam Gopnik, a writer for *The New Yorker* magazine, wrote about his learning curve when he first tried to instant message. His son Nick tutored him that G2G is "got to go," IMHO is "in my humble opinion," BRB is "be right back."

LOL was so obvious, though, Adam didn't need that one translated. It meant Lots of Love. Nick ended every instant message to his Dad with LOL—Adam was touched. Adam sent this loving acronym to everyone who needed it: his sister during her divorce, "We're beside you, LOL;" to his father when he became ill, "LOL."

Soon enough Adam suffers the realization that he's been Laughing

Out Loud at all the wrong times. This is touching to me—it's so funny yet sad too. He's trying to be such a good human and it goes sideways. But that's life, right? A comedy that's tragic sometimes. Or maybe the other way around.

Why do I even bring in this story? You may have noticed already but Listening Out Loud also acronyms out as LOL. As does Live Out Loud. (As do lots of other phrases, I'm sure, that would not line up with my point here. Lost Outside London. Lonely Old Lumberjack. Let's Order Linguini.)

This version of LOL, Listening Out Loud, might be a new approach for you or maybe you knew about it. Either way, now you are aware that superb listening is not about you or your opinions. You can let go of that stress and easily support your conversation partner in thinking through, feeling through, and living through this life together.

You may have ideas you want to share, things you want to say, which, of course, you do. But first the listening; first seek to understand. I know, I know—it'd be easier if everyone just did what we said. But the brain, like the body, needs stretching, yoga-like to stay fit and well. Oh, I like that. Brain yoga. Listening where you are relaxed, attentive, creative, thoughtful and a little stretched.

You are now qualified to engage in exceptionally good conversations. Once you've Listened Out Loud, it could be that it's finally your turn to talk about you. About your ideas, hopes, and plans...

But if your friend doesn't listen well to you, you can just send them right over to me.

Play Date

Go forth with Lots of Luck and Lots of Love to Listen Out Loud, Laugh Out Loud, and Live Out Loud!

Notes and References

Introduction

Kimsey-House, Henry. Kimsey-House, Karen. (2018). *Co-Active Coaching; The Proven Framework for Transformative Conversations at Work and In Life.* (4th edition). Hachette Books. Boston, MA.

Chapter 1

Collins, Jim. (2001). *Good to Great: Why Some Companies Make the Leap and Others Don't.* Harper Business. New York City, NY.

Rogers, Carl R., Farson, Richard E. (2015, Reprint of 1957 edition). *Active Listening.* Martino Publishing. Mansfield Centre, CT.

Chapter 2

Carson, Richard. (2003). *Taming Your Gremlin: A Surprisingly Simple Method for Getting Out of Your Own Way.* HarperCollins Publishers. New York City, NY.

Chamine, Shirzad. (2012). *Positive Intelligence: Why Only 20% of Team and Individuals Achieve their True Potential and How You Can Achieve Yours.* Greenleaf Book Group Press. Austin, TX.

Darst, Cynthia Loy. (2018). *Meet Your inside Team: How to Turn Internal Conflict into Clarity and Move Forward With Your Life.* Team Darst Publishers. Los Angeles, CA.

Chapter 3

Bregman, Rutger. (2020). *Humankind: A Hopeful History.* Little, Brown and Company. New York City, NY.

Chapter 5

Klein, Ezra/ Host. (2021, July 20). "This Conversation Will Change How You Think About Thinking." *The Ezra Klein Show*, The New York Times. https://www.nytimes.com/2021/07/20/podcasts/transcript-ezra-klein-interviews-annie-murphy-paul.html

MacFarquhar, Larissa. (2018, April 2). "The Mind-Expanding Ideas of Andy Clark." The New Yorker Magazine. New York City, NY.

Paul, Annie Murphy. (2021). *The Extended Mind: The Power of Thinking Outside the Brain.* HarperCollins Publishers. New York City, NY.

Chapter 6

Ekman, Paul. Friesen, Wallace V. (2003, Reprint of 1975 edition). *Unmasking The Face: A Guide to Recognizing Emotions from Facial Cues.* Malor Books. San Jose, CA.

Ekman, Paul. (2007). *Emotions Revealed: Recognizing Faces and Feelings to Improve Communication and Emotional Life.* (2nd edition). Henry Holt and Company. New York City, NY.

Chapter 9

Goleman, Daniel. (1995). *Emotional Intelligence: Why It Can Matter More than IQ.* Bantam Books. New York City, NY.

Gottman, John M. (1999, 2015). *The Seven Principles for Making Marriage Work: A Practical Guide from the Country's Foremost Relationship Expert.* Crown Publishing. New York City, NY.

Chapter 10

Abumrad, Jad/ Host. (2011, June 1). "Clever Bots." Radiolab Podcast. Produced by WNYC Studios. https://radiolab.org/episodes/137466-clever-bots

Brown, Brene. (2012). *Daring Greatly: How the Courage to be Vulnerable Transforms the Way We Live, Love, Parent, and Lead.* Penguin Random House. New York City, NY.

Fogg, BJ. (2020). *Tiny Habits: The Small Changes that Change Everything.* Houghton Mifflin Harcourt. New York City, NY.

Chapter 11

Reis, H. T., Lemay, E. P., & Finkenauer, C. (2017). Toward Understanding Understanding: The Importance of Feeling Understood in Relationships. *Social and Personality Psychology Compass, 11*(3), e12308. https://doi.org/10.1111/spc3.12308

Vendantam, Shankar/ Host. (2022, Nov). "Relationship 2.0: What Makes Relationships Thrive?" Hidden Brain Podcast. NPR. https://hiddenbrain.org/podcast/what-makes-relationships-thrive/

Whitmore, John. (2017). *Coaching for Performance: The Principles and Practice of Coaching and Leadership, 25th anniversary edition.* (5th edition). Nicholas Brealey Publishing. London, England.

Chapter 12

Berg, W. J. (2022, September 24). Émile Zola. Encyclopedia Britannica. https://www.britannica.com/biography/Emile-Zola

Gopnik, Adam. (2006, Dec 13.) "LOL." The Moth Radio Hour Podcast. Produced by The Moth and Jay Allison of Atlantic Public Media.

Acknowledgements

A Verse of Gratitude*

There are multitudes for me to thank
Many folk who filled my think tank
Kimcheese & Martha
Co-Actives, Kim, & MARTLA
If not for you this book woulda stank.

*Inspired by Ogden Nash,
American writer (1902-1971)

About the Author

LAUREN POWERS has over 25 years of experience as a renowned executive coach, educator, and change consultant. All over the world, she offers programs in leadership development, team collaboration, and mindset growth. She specializes in powerful, practical, and playful approaches to foster both individual and team growth. Her clients range from big tech and finance firms to small nonprofits, government agencies, and entrepreneurs.

From early childhood, Lauren has been on a quest to understand how humans think, communicate, and make decisions. That fascination led her to earn three undergraduate degrees and a master's from her alma mater, the University of Texas at Austin, but she didn't stop there. Since 1998 Lauren has been on faculty with the Co-Active Training Institute (CTI) and leads the curriculum for training people to become professional coaches. She then went on to become a Master Certified Coach, a designation only 4% of all accredited coaches have achieved.

For Lauren, identifying interpretations, assumptions, and unconscious beliefs are where true transformation begins. Her first book, *The Trouble with Thinking*, explores how our perceptions create our realities and, once that awareness is gained, how we can shift to create new possibilities.

Lauren's bestselling Udemy course on Active Listening has reached a global audience of over 50,000 students and inspired her to write her new book. In *How to Listen Out Loud*, she offers a playful approach to improving listening skills and invites readers to discover how intriguing our fellow humans truly are.

Please visit HowToListenOutLoud.com to learn more or connect with Lauren.

Reviews of Lauren's Udemy Course
Active Listening: You Can Be a Great Listener

"The best course I've ever had. The simple concept, about the two levels of listening, is explored in every section masterfully. Lauren's approach to the subject is engaging and thorough. A great learning experience!"

—Samuel Brito

"I learned a lot about stepping out of being in the ME channel... and that active listening is always about the other person´s channel, not about me and my experiences."

— Marta Boße

"Lauren knocked it out of the park with this class. She helped me uncover why I was encountering dead-end conversations with customers, despite my enthusiasm and attempts at engagement. Lauren gave me the tools to learn to speak and connect with level two listening skills. My blind spots are removed, and I feel empowered to listen deeply and show my customers that I genuinely care. Thank you, Lauren—I'm buying your book ASAP!"

—Angel D.

"In this course I got amazing insights into the mechanics of how to enrich conversations —and my life. It gives you all you need to know to make future conversations more meaningful, respectful, and personal. Thank you, Lauren, for sharing this wonderful gift with us. Becoming a level 2 listener is a transformative process. It makes you understand the world and other people differently."

— Fabian Beranovsky

"The insights Lauren shared are very good and very helpful in day-to-day life. Active listening not only grows you professionally but emotionally too, and it helps you to be the best version of yourself."

— Pratyush Singh

For more information on this course, visit
https://www.udemy.com/course/active-listening-you-can-be-a-great-listener